D0368760

FACTORS IN GERMAN HISTORY

FACTORS
IN
GERMAN HISTORY

BY

G. BARRACLOUGH

Oriel and Merton Colleges, Oxford
St. John's College, Cambridge
Professor in the University
of Liverpool

275390

Connetquot Public Library
760 Ocean Avenue
Bohemia, New York 11716

GREENWOOD PRESS, PUBLISHERS
WESTPORT, CONNECTICUT

Library of Congress Cataloging in Publication Data

Barraclough, Geoffrey, 1908-
  Factors in German history.

  Reprint of the 1946 ed. published by B. Blackwell,
Oxford.
  Includes index.
  1. Germany--History.   I.   Title.
DD89.B25   1979   943   78-21483
ISBN 0-313-21066-7

First published 1946 by Basil Blackwell, Oxford

Reprinted with the permission of Basil Blackwell Publisher

Reprinted in 1979 by Greenwood Press, Inc.
51 Riverside Avenue, Westport, CT 06880

Printed in the United States of America

10 9 8 7 6 5 4 3 2 1

CONTENTS

MAPS

PREFACE

IN 1933 a German historian published some lectures with the challenging title: *Germany's Middle Ages — Germany's Destiny*.[1] In so doing he put his finger on a cardinal element in German history which has never been appreciated at its face value in all the many attempts, in England and elsewhere, to explain the history of Germany in terms of nineteenth-century industrialism, twentieth-century imperialism and the European balance of power as it has evolved since the Congress of Vienna in 1815. All these factors play their part, often a big part, in the evolution of modern Germany towards the revolution of 1933 and the disaster of 1945; but neither the development nor the physiognomy nor the problem of modern Germany will be understood unless we are aware of the living German past enshrined in the German present.

The present volume is an attempt, having set forth briefly the constituent factors which were the legacy of Germany's middle ages, to trace their influence in moulding German destinies from the dawn of the modern era to the present day. It draws largely, and without acknowledgment or apology, on my fuller survey of German history, *The Origins of Modern Germany* (Oxford: Basil Blackwell, 1946). Two reasons above all others have led me to supplement the larger volume by the shorter outline which follows: first, a belief that it is important to place the basic facts before the largest possible public; secondly, a desire to make the conclusions of the longer work available in a form in which they can readily reach the younger, growing generation in the schools. But I hope that many who have read the pages which follow will turn thereafter to the fuller version, for the extraordinary fluctuations of German fortunes through the ages are a story, exciting and engrossing in itself, which vitally concerns us all to-day, and on a proper understanding of which our future peace and happiness may well depend.

G. BARRACLOUGH

March 1st, 1946

---

[1] H. Heimpel, *Deutschlands Mittelalter Deutschlands Schicksal* (Freiburger Universitätsreden, no. 12), Freiburg im Breisgau, 1933.

FACTORS IN GERMAN HISTORY

Chapter I

THE MEDIAEVAL BACKGROUND
(213-1356)

§ 1. *The Settlement of the Germanic Peoples in Western Europe* (213-511)

BACK in the third century after Christ, when the pulse of
Roman civilization was already slackening, Europe became
the scene of a mass-migration of peoples, pressing from east
to west across the frontiers of the Roman empire along the Rhine
and Danube. This vast movement of displacement which took over
two centuries to complete, transformed the physiognomy of Europe;
it introduced new stock, new social forms and new perspectives, and
placed western Europe under new masters; it shattered the framework of the Mediterranean civilization then existing, and created the
mould from which western European civilization was to spring.
Roman provincial life, swamped under the influx of new peoples
driven forward from the Baltic and the Vistula under the pressure
of the barbarians from the steppes of central Asia, gave way to new
societies and the cohesion of the empire collapsed: thus was formed
the matrix of a new civilization with its axis in the west.

When, in the second half of the fifth century, the pressure from
the east relaxed, and the invading peoples secured a respite to consolidate and organize their hold, the shape of a new Europe was
visible. Some of the peoples had pressed forward as far as the western
seaboard of Europe; some had even moved beyond. The Vandals,
roaming wide from their home on the shores of the Baltic, had
passed through Gaul and Spain into Africa; Angles and Saxons from
Schleswig and Holstein had crossed the North Sea and settled in
Britain. In Spain the Visigoths had followed the Vandals; the Ostro-
goths were established in Italy. Behind them other peoples poured
through the breach they had made; the Alemannians, the Burgundians and the Franks followed the Vandals across the Rhine into
Gaul, while the territories between Rhine and Elbe were occupied
by Frisians, Saxons and Thuringians; farther south the Alemannians
and a tribe from Bohemia, the *Boii*, disputed the Bavarian plain.

Eastern Germany beyond the Elbe and Bohemia were left vacant for the infiltration of Slavonic tribes, pressing forward across the Oder from their homes north of the Carpathians.

It is with the history of the easternmost of the Germanic tribes, whose migrations changed the ethnography of western Europe—the Frisians, Saxons, Franks, Thuringians, Alemannians (or Swabians) and Bavarians, inhabitants of the territories along the Slav border-land from the Elbe and the line of the Bohemian forest to the Danube and the eastern Alps — that the following pages are concerned. Down to the twelfth century, when expansion and colonization on a wide front carried the frontiers of Germany far to the east and led to the absorption into the German stock of many peoples of Slav blood, the six peoples enumerated above constituted the human material of German history. They were distinguished in three ways from most other peoples of the age of migration. First, they were of all the Germanic peoples those which had maintained the closest contact with their original homes; they had expanded rather than migrated. Secondly, as the easternmost of the stocks, they were exposed to further incursions and could never be oblivious of the need for keeping watch and ward along their eastern frontiers. Thirdly, their contacts with the decaying civilization of Rome were few, and many of them (particularly east of the Rhine) inhabited lands which had never undergone Roman political organization. They lived in the ramparts and outworks of the new Europe, a land with few cities and little trace of urban civilization; they hated the Roman towns — 'walled tombs', as they described them[1] — and, unlike the peoples farther west, made little attempt to adapt their mode of life to the social conditions of the Roman provinces. An exception were the Franks. The Salian Franks, forcing a passage through the weak Roman defences near the estuary of the Rhine, spread rapidly in the fourth and fifth centuries into Gaul north of the Loire; the Ripuarian and Hessian Franks (Chatti) spread out from the area round Cologne into the valleys of the Main and Moselle and westwards towards the Eifel and the Ardennes. Here both groups came into contact with Roman life and Roman provincial organization, and finally, in the days of Clovis (485-511), the Salian Franks stepped into the Roman inheritance. In 486 Clovis ousted and slew the

---

[1] Cf. R. Koebner, 'The Settlement and Colonization of Europe', *Cambr. Econ. Hist.*, I (1941), 23.

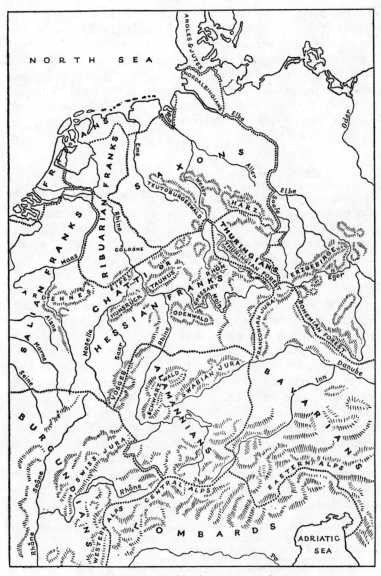

The Lands settled by the German peoples.

Roman, Syagrius, and established his rule over the Gallic population between the Loire and the Somme; at the same time he united the Frankish people, hitherto divided into a large number of petty tribes, under his dynasty. By 511 a new force had arrived on the scene, which was to dominate European history for upward of four centuries: the Frankish monarchy, creator of the Frankish empire, was set on the road which made it, by the time of Charles the Great, ruler of Europe from the Atlantic to the Adriatic and from the Pyrenees to the Elbe.

§ 2. *The German Peoples in the Frankish Empire* (511-918)

It was through the efforts of the Frankish kings, pursued through many generations, that the German peoples were slowly reduced to political unity. Like all other nations of modern Europe, the Germans appeared on the threshold of history as a number of separate and often hostile stems, and a sense of common nationality and unity was only very gradually attained, as a consequence of subjection within a single political framework imposed by strong and predatory kings. In this respect German history is no different from that of England or France.[1] What united the German peoples was subjection, through long generations, to the Frankish monarchy. The sons of Clovis conquered the Burgundian kingdom in 532 and subjected Thuringia to Frankish rule, colonizing the region between the Main and the Thuringian forest, which thus became known as Franconia; the Saxons to the north became tributaries; the Bavarians recognized Frankish hegemony. Later, in the eighth century, after a period of decline under the later Merovingians, the work of unification was renewed by the Carolingian dynasty, which gradually reduced the provinces to submission again, replacing provincial leaders (dukes) by officers of the Frankish crown (counts). The Swabian dukedom was suppressed in 730 by Charles Martel; Thuringia was brought under direct royal control in 741; the Bavarian dukedom was

---

[1] It is important to emphasize this fact because the disunity apparent in German history between the fourteenth and the nineteenth centuries has often been attributed to the existence of racial or 'tribal' disparities unknown elsewhere. Bryce, *The Holy Roman Empire* (ed. 1928), 424, was nearer to the truth when he wrote: 'The want of national union and political liberty from which Germany used to suffer need not be attributed to the differences of her races; for, conspicuous as that difference was in the days of Otto the Great, it was less conspicuous than in France, where intruding Franks, Goths, Burgundians and Northmen were mingled with primitive Celts and Basques; less conspicuous than in Spain, or Italy, or Britain.'

destroyed by Charles the Great after the rebellion of Duke Tassilo III in 788. Finally in a series of bitter wars lasting from 772 to 804 Charles the Great subdued Saxony, uprooted thousands of Saxons from their homes, and destroyed the native political institutions of the Saxon people. The eastern lands beyond the Rhine were administered in the interests of the Frankish monarchy by Frankish counts and a uniform system of government was imposed.

This uniform system of Frankish government constituted an enduring element in the political heritage of Germany in the early middle ages. But it would be a serious error to exaggerate its effectiveness. Gaul, or France, in the west and Germany in the east were both subjected to Frankish administrative organization; but beneath the uniformity imposed by the crown there were many differences of tradition and social structure. In Gaul, the Franks stepped into and remoulded the Roman legacy of provincial government; in the east, they had to deal with peoples who had not yet reached the stage of monarchical rule. Furthermore, while there was a continuous Christian tradition in the west, the advent of Christianity east of the Rhine reached back (apart from Bavaria) only to the days of the Anglo-Saxon missions at the beginning of the eighth century. The conversion of the Frisians was due to the Anglo-Saxon, Willibrord (696-739); the revival of Christianity in Alemannia was the work of Pirmin, who founded the abbey of Reichenau on Lake Constance in 724; the conversion of the Hessians and Thuringians was the work of the greatest missionary of all, Wynfrith or Boniface, whose activity, beginning in 718, culminated in the foundation of the great monastic centre of Fulda in 744. But the conversion of the Saxons and the organization of a Christian church in Saxony only occurred under Charles the Great, as part of the campaign for the subjection of the Saxon people, and was imposed by force. Both the civil and the ecclesiastical organization introduced by the Carolingians into the eastern provinces of the Frankish empire had, therefore, by comparison with the west, shallow roots. In Gaul the county organization, indurated since the sixth century, had become the territorial framework of administration, and the country was divided into counties which were units of local government; in the east, where the count was little more than the alien agent of Frankish domination, a royal commissioner appointed to enforce and maintain Frankish rule over a conquered people, it was more fragile, and a complete network of counties was never created. East of the Rhine, in short, the Franks had not time to complete their work of political organization; Frankish institutions did not take root and earlier institutions and social groupings were not obliterated.

The effect of these deeper differences, hidden under the surface so long as Charles the Great lived, were felt after his death in 814, and became increasingly marked in the second half of the ninth century, when a new wave of barbarian invasions swept over Europe. Dissension and strife within the ruling dynasty weakened Carolingian government under Charles the Great's son, Louis (814-840), and resulted in the partition of the empire in 843. But the famous treaty of Verdun (843) and the division between the west Frankish (or French) and the east Frankish (or German) territories which it marked, were the result not of racial or provincial differences, but simply of dynastic conflicts within the royal house.[1] What really destroyed the unity of the empire was pressure from outside — the pressure of Danish, Magyar and Saracen invaders breaking in from north and east and south. Once again the strain of invasion and constant warfare, with its trail of devastation, retrogression cultural and economic, and depopulation, reduced Europe to anarchy. Thrown back on local resources for withstanding the onslaught, subject to varying degrees of pressure from without, the different provinces of the Carolingian empire each reacted in its own way to the invaders; and the characteristic reactions of each modified the political and social structure, calling forth new and reawakening old forces. When after more than a century the barbarian threat was thrown off, the face of Europe had changed. The uniformity of Carolingian government perished; the fundamental differences between the social and political organization of France, Germany and Italy were reasserted; and the east Frankish lands entered on the course of independent development by which they were transformed from an integral part of the Frankish empire into a separate German kingdom.

The independent development which set in about the middle of the ninth century reflected the earlier history of the regions concerned. In France the county organization proved its strength and

[1] The idea that the unity of the Frankish realm was destroyed through inherent divergencies between the nationalities was refuted by G. Monod, 'Du rôle de l'opposition des races et des nationalités dans la dissolution de l'empire carolingien', *Annuaire de l'École des Hautes-Études*, 1896.

durability, and the counts, who were the backbone of resistance to the invaders, increased their political power at the expense of the monarchy. By the beginning of the tenth century French society had broken into some thirty distinct territorial divisions, and the foundations were laid for the rapid growth of French feudalism. In Germany the preconditions for such a development were lacking. The county organization was too weak to become the framework of a new society, and instead there was a recrudescence of the political divisions which Carolingian government had sought to sweep away. Instead of the establishment of thirty to forty small territorial units, as in France, the period of Viking and Magyar invasion saw in Germany (excluding Lorraine) the rise of five great duchies: Franconia, Saxony, Thuringia, Swabia and Bavaria. Instead of the growth of feudalism, as a source of social cohesion and a means of combating the invaders, German society — still in the main a society of free men and free peasants — regrouped around the military leaders of the eastern marches, the *duces* or dukes, who asserted themselves in resistance to the Danes and Magyars. The duchy, which thus became an important factor in German political life, was 'a revolutionary authority' justified only by the stress of the times;[1] the barbarian invasions and the military necessities they created placed new power in the hands of the military leaders and the guardians of the frontiers, enabling — or perhaps compelling — them to extend their sway, until finally they assumed authority throughout the length and breadth of the province. By the end of the ninth century, when the Frankish dynasty petered out in the person of the illegitimate Carolingian, Arnulf (887-899), and his son, Louis the Child (899-911), the dukes who had begun as military leaders under the crown were on the way to political independence, and it looked between 899 and 918 as though the east Frankish lands might go the way of the Lotharingian 'Middle Kingdom' and break up into a number of petty states. The Franconian duke, Conrad, elected king in 911, was with difficulty able to maintain himself or to secure the loyalty of the other dukes, and it seemed as if, with the extinction of the Carolingian dynasty, the only bond of unity between the German lands had perished. The future of Germany, hardly yet existing save as part of the crumbling Carolingian empire, hung in the balance.

---

[1] 'Eine revolutionäre Gewalt, die nur in dem Drang der Zeitumstände ihre Berechtigung fand'; Giesebrecht, *Geschichte der deutschen Kaiserzeit*, I (1881), 806.

B

§ 3. *The Rise of the German Monarchy and the Consolidation of German Unity* (919-1075)

The question in German history in 919 was whether the Frankish inheritance of unity or the ancient tribal divisions, revived under the pressure of war and invasion, would triumph; it was the question of retrogression or of further progress along the lines laid down by the Carolingian dynasty. This question was decided in all essentials by the Saxon kings who ruled Germany between 919 and 1002. Ruling not as Saxons but as Franks, they defeated ducal strivings for autonomy, and maintained and built up their Frankish inheritance. In a long struggle Henry I (919-936) and Otto I (936-973) broke down the resistance of the dukes, and the issue was decided when, after four years of bitter contest, Otto II (973-983) finally overcame the opposition of duke Henry of Bavaria.

Many factors contributed to the royal success. The very fact that the dukes had risen as military leaders in time of war set limits to their power. By taking the lead in resisting the Hungarian incursions and defending the eastern frontiers, Henry I and Otto I deprived the dukes of one source of authority and definitely established their own superiority. Otto the Great's famous victory over the Hungarians at the battle of the Lech in 955 not only marked the end of the Magyar threat but also gave the monarchy the upper hand at home; further prestige was won by Otto I's victories over the Slavonic tribes along the Elbe and the extension of Germany's frontiers to the east. On this basis of material success the monarchy was able to revive the traditions and methods of Frankish government. Here again the position of the Saxon kings was advantageous; for weak as were the foundations which the east Frankish rulers left for the German kings of the Saxon dynasty, they were strong by comparison with the basis on which the wielders of ducal power had to build. The inheritance of the dukes went back to the dark days of the dying ninth century; the inheritance of the German kings reached back to the height of the Carolingian monarchy. Carolingian traditions played a large part in Ottonian policy, and their maintenance was one main reason why Germany was the first of all the lands springing from the old Frankish empire to recover from the ravages of the Danish, Saracen and Magyar invasions. In particular, Otto I revived the old connexion between church and monarchy which had been a main pillar of Carolingian government since the days of St. Boniface. A natural community of interests bound together the clergy, who looked to the king as *rex et sacerdos*, the divinely appointed ruler of church and state, and the crown against the dukes, whose tendency it was to reduce the churches in their lands to subservience; and from the time of Otto I the bishops and clergy were privileged and raised up as a counterpoise to the dukes. Carolingian tradition also played its part in Ottonian foreign policy. Lorraine, which on the extinction of the east Frankish dynasty in 911 had wavered in its allegiance, was reunited in 925. The connexion with Italy, which had its roots in a common past in the Carolingian empire, was also maintained; between Arnulf, crowned emperor at Rome in 896, and Otto the Great, crowned emperor at Rome in 962, there was no essential breach. Henry I was on the point of leading an expedition to Rome at the time of his death in 936; the duke of Swabia was killed on an Italian expedition in 926, and the duke of Bavaria entered Lombardy in 934 with the idea of winning a crown for his son. Otto the Great's Italian policy therefore denoted not (as often said) a 'revival' of the empire but the maintenance of existing tendencies. On the one side, it was in line with his policy of checking the ambitions of the south German dukes, whose pursuit of an independent foreign policy was a threat to royal supremacy;[1] on the other side, it was part and parcel of the Carolingian traditions on which Ottonian rule was based.

The foundation of the Ottonian empire in 962 marked the emergence of Germany from the period of retrogression which had set in with the barbarian invasions about the middle of the ninth century. The basis of royal power was still in Germany, and Rome played a small part in Ottonian calculations; but the coronation of the German king as emperor marked the establishment of German hegemony in Europe, due to the rapidity of its recovery from the setbacks of the ninth century. While France under the later Carolingians was sinking deeper into feudal anarchy, Germany was set on the road to recovery. Already under the year 920 the records mention the *regnum Teutonicorum*, indicating that even at this early date a consciousness of the unity of the five German peoples was in

---

[1] 'A German king,' it has been well said, 'who wished to prevent the pursuit of an independent Italian policy by Swabia or Bavaria, was of necessity driven to pursue an Italian policy of his own'; cf. H. Heimpel, 'Bemerkungen zur Geschichte König Heinrichs des Ersten', *Sächsische Akademie der Wissenschaften, phil.-hist. Klasse*, LXXXVIII (1936), iv. 45.

existence. The restoration of peaceful conditions and the strengthening of the monarchy under Otto the Great quickly made this unity a reality. Economic recovery, following on pacification, led to intensive internal colonization and land reclamation, through which geographical obstacles to unity (e.g. the Franconian Jura, the Spessart, and the Rhön, separating northern and southern Germany) were overcome. The consolidation of the connexion between Germany and Italy and German control of the Alpine passes brought a revival of commerce and the first stirrings of town life. Helped by the church, the Saxon monarchy attacked the current regionalism. The great bishops and abbots of Saxon times, travelling the country in the services of Christianity or king, broke down provincial boundaries, particularly the boundaries between south Germany and the Saxon north, and new monastic centres quickly raised Saxony to the same level of civilization as Swabia or Bavaria. This work of cultural advance is particularly associated with the name of Henry II (1002-1024), a ruler of deep religious convictions, for whom the conscientious exercise of his sacerdotal prerogatives was the first duty of a king; as a result of his efforts regional differences fell into the background, and in the course of the eleventh century the collective name for the German people, *Teutonici*, rapidly became usual.

Under the Salian dynasty, which succeeded to the Saxon inheritance in 1024, we can trace a conscious attempt to translate the progress of the previous century into political terms. Conrad II (1024-1039), Henry III (1039-1056) and Henry IV (1056-1106) sought each in his own way to capitalize the new resources opening up, to mobilize the new rising classes behind the monarchy, and to adapt the machinery of government to the new conditions. Gradually under the Salian kings a great programme of administrative reform took shape, designed to free the monarchy from reliance on the aristocracy and on the church and to place royal government on durable foundations. Its keynote was the development and regular exploitation of the crown lands, the use of the 'ministerial' class, and centralization. The *ministeriales*, whose services were the backbone of the Salian programme, had sprung in Saxon times from the upper ranks of the dependent classes, and with the recovery of agriculture and the requirements of estate-management had quickly risen to importance; because of their traditions of obedience and dependence they were more tractable than vassals and less dangerous to entrust with power. Hence they rapidly assumed an important place on church estates, and from the time of Conrad II they were assigned similar functions on the demesnes of the crown. Conrad II was the first German ruler to favour the *ministeriales* as a class and to organize them into an administrative staff; Werner, his chief *ministerialis*, was in his capacity of supervisor of the fisc a kind of chief intendant or comptroller-general, the earliest secular minister in German history. Even more notable was Benno, who rose rapidly in Henry III's service, became mayor of the imperial palace at Goslar, chief administrator of the crown lands, and was selected for the bishopric of Osnabrück in 1054. To men such as these was entrusted the execution of the Salian programme of administrative reform. They had the task of managing and consolidating the crown estates, and so successful were their efforts that by the death of Conrad II in 1039 the material wealth of the monarchy was greater than ever before. In 1064-1065 an inventory of crown lands and of services owed was drawn up, anticipating by twenty years the Domesday Survey of England; inquests were held and proprietors were forced to produce their titles; royal rights and impositions, which had been exacted from freemen in Carolingian times but had since passed into desuetude, were revived; the royal monopoly over the forest was reaffirmed, the king not only laying claim to unappropriated forest and waste land, but also subjecting the inhabitants, who had settled the land as 'squatters', to the control of royal officers. But Salian policy went beyond recuperation, revindication and reform. Under Henry IV the systematic exploitation of the crown lands became the basis of a concrete plan for a centralized monarchy with a permanent capital at Goslar in the Harz mountains. Henry III had built a fortress at Goslar; Henry IV deliberately set out to cover the Saxon and Thuringian countryside with a network of castles garrisoned by loyal Swabian *ministeriales* from the Salian estates in southern Germany. In the vicinity of Goslar were the famous Rammelsberg silver mines, discovered in the reign of Otto I, capable of providing the king with a steady supply of bullion and thus freeing him from the necessity of remunerating servants and adherents with grants of land. With increased economic resources and on the sure foundation of a money economy, Henry IV's object was to enhance the crown's authority by building up its landed properties and securing a steady and permanent revenue, while behind the whole programme was the energy and devoted service of the royal *ministeriales*, whose task it was to execute the king's plans.

Such was, in brief, the position in 1075. Taking all in all, it was a ruthless and ambitious programme, bound to meet opposition; but it was also a statesmanlike project, revealing Henry IV's keen sense of the potentialities of the situation. Germany had far outstripped France and England in the pace of its recovery and was already on the path leading to more modern forms of government; indeed, Henry IV's policy between 1065 and 1075 compares more readily with that of Henry II of England in the twelfth century than with that of his English contemporary, William the Conqueror. Had his success proved durable, it is scarcely doubtful that Henry IV would have created a great German state coeval with Norman England and anticipating the French monarchy of Philip Augustus; from that era we should date the beginning of new forms of government in Germany and a new concentration of German national powers behind the monarchy. But at this juncture a crisis intervened which destroyed all Henry IV's early plans for the establishment of a strong, centralized monarchy, and irrevocably changed the forms of government and social texture of Germany. In 1076 a new chapter opened in German history. The constructive work of the monarchy was challenged in a struggle which, lasting close on half a century, shook the political structure of Germany to its foundations. When in 1122 the Concordat of Worms brought the struggle to an end, a new Germany had arisen, as little like Germany at the time of Henry III's death in 1056 as that Germany resembled the country in which, in 919, the Saxon dynasty began its work of consolidation and unification.

§ 4. *Revolution and Reaction* (1076–1152)

The work of the Salian dynasty between 1024 and 1075 was not destined to last. In spite of the remarkable progress achieved in the eleventh century, there were still serious problems outstanding, which became accentuated during the long minority between 1056 and 1065 with which Henry IV's reign opened. Although the power of the dukes had been broken, thanks to the efforts of the Ottonian dynasty, Saxony and Lorraine were still centres of unrest, the latter due to its proximity to France, the former in reaction to Salian policy, which seemed to threaten the privileges of the Saxon freemen and to betoken subjection to the yoke of a centralized monarchical government. At the same time economic recovery, the opening up of new land and the work of colonization, had strengthened the position of the aristocracy, which (unlike the aristocracy of France) had escaped the bonds of feudalism and prized its 'liberties'; its prerogatives were threatened by Salian policy, particularly by the reliance which the Salian kings placed on the ministerial class, and so it gradually moved into open opposition to the crown. Another factor was the recovery of the church, the growing strength of the papacy, which was determined to exert full control over the bishops and metropolitans of the national churches and was no longer willing to accord the monarchy a quasi-sacerdotal position. Already in the days of Pope Leo IX (1048-1054), links had been formed between the German aristocracy and Rome; and on Leo's death the next two popes were nominees of Godfrey of Lorraine, the most unruly of Henry III's vassals. In these circumstances it is not surprising that the papacy used its opportunity during Henry IV's minority to shake off imperial tutelage. The party of clerical reform, with its programme of free elections and the abolition of royal investitures, now assumed control in Rome. Such a programme was inevitably unacceptable to the monarchy, not only in Germany but also in France and England; for the crown had placed much of the administration in the hands of the episcopate and could not afford to see the bishops emancipated from royal control.[1] Hence a conflict with the papacy became inevitable, and in the case of Henry IV it assumed major proportions because of the imperial connexion between Germany and Italy, which now became a funereal entanglement involving the German king in an out-and-out war which he might otherwise have escaped.

It was the combination of these different factors that led, after 1075, to a fundamental challenge to the whole policy of the Salian dynasty. Already in 1070 and 1073 serious rebellions had broken out in Saxony, in which the aristocracy and the free peasantry had united against the crown; but they were ruthlessly crushed by Henry IV. At the end of 1075 a new opponent entered the lists, rallying the elements of German opposition. Under the leadership

---

[1] According to J. W. Thompson, *Feudal Germany* (1928), 135, by 1073 no less than fifty-three counties in Germany were in the hands of the episcopate.

of Gregory VII (1073-1085), the papacy declared war on the German emperor and on the whole established system of German imperialism. In 1076 Gregory excommunicated and deposed Henry, and joined forces with the south German and Saxon opposition, which saw in the movement of church reform and the papal attack on Henry IV a useful instrument for the assertion of aristocratic privileges against the centralizing policy of the monarchy. In October 1076 at the Diet of Tribur Henry IV was confronted by a united clerical and aristocratic opposition and was forced to capitulate; and when in mid-winter he fled to Italy seeking reconciliation with the pope, the German princes proceeded to the last step and at Forchheim on March 13th, 1077, elected a new king, Rudolf of Swabia.

The struggle which broke out in 1076 lasted for a whole generation until Henry IV's death in 1106. The death of the anti-king, Rudolf, in 1080, brought no appeasement, nor even the death of Gregory VII in 1085; for the struggle was not a mere clash of personalities. What was at issue was the whole position and policy of the German monarchy and therewith the character of the German constitution. What Gregory and his partisans attacked was the hereditary monarchy, which had raised Germany and Italy out of the anarchy of the ninth and tenth centuries; they challenged the monarchy by divine right, consecrated like the priestly office and confided to the guidance and arbitrament of God alone. For Gregory the king was a removable official, who only remained king so long as he performed his duties; and it rested with the pope, as successor of Peter and vicar of Christ, to determine when a ruler was acting as a just king, when he was a tyrant who must be removed. Furthermore, the king must be chosen as a lord would choose a bailiff. Not God's will, inscrutably manifest in the virtues of royal blood, was to decide who should rule, but practical tests of suitability or *idoneitas*; and it was the task of the lay princes to select and put forward for papal approval a candidate whose suitability was proven. The Gregorian theory of kingship therefore culminated, in the political sphere, in a theory of election and of elective monarchy; for hereditary succession gave no guarantee of *idoneitas* — on the contrary, as Innocent III was later to affirm, it was a presumption against suitability. This theory, which found practical expression in the election of Rudolf of Swabia in 1077, admirably suited the interests of the German princes; for it implied that the real source of authority in the kingdom lay in the princes who elected the king. In the pope's view, the princes, not the king, were the representatives of the kingdom; and the ultimate result of the incidents of 1076 and 1077 was, therefore, the establishment of a political order in which the king, with his royal rights, stood opposed to the princes, who represented — or claimed to represent — the interests of the kingdom against the king. It was the beginning of that 'dualism' between king and princes, between nation and principalities, which was to prove the curse of German history down to the nineteenth century.

In enunciating the theory of elective monarchy, Gregory VII threw a flaming brand into Germany. The Saxon and Salian kings had saved Germany from the conflicts and turmoil of disputed elections, by instituting the sound practice of hereditary succession, which made possible a real continuity of policy, and was thus the foundation for a progressive evolution of government. After 1077, the curse of elective monarchy again descended on Germany. Lothar II (1125-1137) and Conrad III (1138-1152), both elected in opposition to the hereditary claimant, were crippled throughout their reigns by the concessions they were forced to make in order to secure election. But the result of the contest which broke out in 1076 was not merely to weaken the monarchy, but also to strengthen the position of the German aristocracy. The long period of civil war during the last thirty years of Henry IV's reign profoundly modified the texture of German society. Devastation, famine and rapine ruined the free classes, particularly the peasantry, while the unsettled times created a new demand for armed knights. The result was a rapid spread of feudalism, hitherto a negligible factor in German social history, which enabled the princes to build up their followings and extend their sway over the population. Feudal castles sprang up everywhere in response to the need for protection, and the castellany became the unit of administration. The monarchy, its hands tied by the struggle with the papacy, could neither undertake the major tasks of government itself nor prevent the princes undertaking them in their territories without its assent. The confusion, anarchy and lack of a universally recognized authority, which prevailed for a generation after 1075, in conjunction with the decline of the free classes, led to a disintegration of government; old administrative units and boundaries disappeared, and when after a generation peace was restored to the land, new units of government had taken their place. During the period when royal authority was weak and disputed, the aristocracy on its own initiative took charge and remodelled the administrative machinery in accordance with its own interests and with the strengthened position it had secured through the spread of feudalism. From the beginning of the twelfth century we find the German aristocracy referring to their lands as *terrae suae*, while they themselves were described as *domini terrae*; and these terms, implying territorial lordship, reflected the increase in the powers of the aristocracy, who profited from the contest between the crown and the papacy to reject the tightening bonds of royal control which Henry IV's early policy had foreshadowed, and to assert their predominance in German political society.

If we review the results of the period 1076-1152, we see two sets of facts, each of weighty consequence for the future. On the one hand, the old foundations of royal government were undermined; on the other hand, a major shift in the distribution of political power laid the foundations for a new constitution, the character of which was to be aristocratic rather than monarchical. The weakening of the monarchy was evident, first of all, in the emergence of the elective principle and in the acceptance by Henry V (1106-1125) of the view that the king was only *primus inter pares*, the first of the princes, ruling less by hereditary right than on the basis of a revocable contract or engagement entered into with the princes, which left them the whiphand.[1] It was accentuated by the dissipation and wastage of the crown lands, partly through the devastation of the civil wars, partly by lavish grants to secure adherents, in consequence of which the material basis of royal power was destroyed. Finally, the loosening of the bonds between church and state deprived the monarchy in large measure of the services of the bishops and clergy, which had contributed so greatly to the progress achieved under the Saxon and Salian kings. The old pillars of the Salian monarchy had gone. The church was feudalized, the bishops no longer implicitly loyal to the crown; after the Concordat of Worms, which in 1122 brought to

---

[1] This attitude — contrasting radically with that of Henry IV — found expression in the characteristic statement made by Henry V at the very beginning of his reign: 'The removal of a single person,' he said, 'even if he is the supreme head of the state, is a reparable injury to the realm, but the destruction of the princes is the destruction of the very kingdom.' Cf. A Degener, 'Die Erhebung Heinrichs V. und das Herzogtum Sachsen', *Mitteilungen des österr. Instituts für Geschichtsforschung*, Erg.-Bd. XIV (1939), 136.

an end the conflict with the papacy, the efforts of the episcopate were increasingly concentrated on building up their territorial power, and their new territorial interests threw them in large measure on to the side of the princes and feudatories. From 1106 to 1152 the latter were in the ascendant, consolidating what they had won in the civil wars between 1076 and 1106. This consolidation of princely power was a momentous factor in German history. In establishing new units of territorial government, the princes created the nuclei from which the German principalities of late mediaeval and modern times were to spring. Many generations were to pass before the principalities took shape and the princes established full territorial control; but already at the beginning of the twelfth century the great aristocratic families were mounting the path leading to territorial sovereignty. The powers asserted by the princes under Henry IV were the basis of their later *Landeshoheit*, and it was the conflict of his reign, and the revolutionary social changes it inaugurated, which gave them the opportunity to assert and consolidate these powers. This was the outstanding contribution of the period to Germany's future: in the civil wars loosed by Pope Gregory VII we have to seek the beginnings of the territorial disunity, of the fantastic map of German particularism and of the unlimited sovereignty of the princes, which dominated German history from the fourteenth to the nineteenth centuries.

§ 5. Germany under the Hohenstaufen: the Rise and Fall of the Hohenstaufen Empire (1152–1250)

It would be difficult to exaggerate the setback to the development of Germany resulting from the events of 1076–1152. Up to that time German political development had been healthy, full of promise for the future, and in most respects ahead of that of the other countries of Europe. Inevitably there was opposition on the part of vested interests to the centralizing and unifying work of the monarchy; but until 1075 there was every indication that the crown would triumph over these reactionary elements, particularly as it could look for support to the rising towns. The intervention of the papacy, forcing Henry IV to wage war on two fronts, threw the achievements of the previous century into the melting-pot; by giving new strength to the elements of opposition in Germany, it transformed the whole situation to the detriment of the monarchy, and the future, hitherto bright and promising, became problematical. Nevertheless, there were still a number of factors favouring the monarchy, once the conflict with the church was settled in 1122. It had the benefit of long tradition, which was strengthened when, as the twelfth century proceeded, a widespread reaction set in against the anarchy of the previous generation and an insistent demand arose for a restoration of effective government and a reconstruction of German society on stable foundations. If the civil wars under Henry IV had led to a dissolution of the old society, they also released new springs of political action and inaugurated a process of social and political reconstruction; and it was still possible that the new forces, controlled by the crown, would provide a new foundation for royal power, instead of contributing to the consolidation of princely power. From 1106 to 1152 superior control was lacking and events favoured the princes; but for a ruler capable of adapting his policy to the new conditions and of building on new foundations, the situation was not hopeless.

Such a ruler Germany found in Frederick I of Hohenstaufen (1152-1190), who takes his place alongside Henry II of England and Philip Augustus of France as one of the great constructive statesmen of the middle ages. Frederick quickly saw the hopelessness of attempting to revive the Salian methods of government, and instead accepted the new state of affairs and set himself the task of reducing it to order. His fundamental object in Germany was to subordinate to the purposes of government the inchoate feudalism which had sprung up between 1076 and 1152 and on this basis to create an organized and integrated feudal state. Such a form of government was very different from the centralization which Henry IV had sought to introduce; but it represented the maximum that was possible in the new circumstances. Conscious of the loss of power which the monarchy had suffered between 1076 and 1152, and unable to count on an adequate material basis for government within Germany itself, Frederick set out to retrieve the position by developing the resources and prerogatives of the imperial monarchy in Italy. For a Swabian ruler, whose territorial power lay almost exclusively in southern Germany, this was a natural policy. Geographically, Swabia was as close to Burgundy and Italy as it was to

the rest of Germany; and from the beginning of his reign we find
Frederick exploiting the advantages of this position, and developing
Swabian connexions to the south and south-west. The result was
that Italy played a greater part in Frederick's calculations than in
those of any of his predecessors on the German throne; and it has
sometimes been held that his policy sacrificed Germany to Italy and
that the energies he devoted to Italy would better have been spent
in Germany. We shall see that this charge can reasonably be levelled
against his successors on the German throne; but in the case of
Frederick I it cannot be sustained. After the losses inflicted on the
monarchy between 1076 and 1152, it was only by mobilizing the
resources of Italy that recovery was possible.[1] Furthermore, by
building up his power in Swabia and Burgundy and Lombardy,
Frederick could hope to secure possession of a central stronghold, an
effective basis of government from which he could reach out to
control Saxony in the north, Bavaria and Austria in the east, and
Tuscany and central Italy in the south. Frederick's conception of
his position seems to have been that of a feudal monarch, firmly
established on his own central demesnes, exercising feudal suzerainty
in a state which was a federation of feudal principalities. The
monarchy had no longer the resources to exercise direct control of
outlying provinces, particularly in north and east Germany, which
were left to the princes; but the latter were held in check by feudal
bonds. Frederick's government envisaged a real measure of co-
operation between the crown and the princes. After the shattering
blows to royal power in the previous generation, the monarchy
could not undertake the work of reconstruction single-handed, and
wide powers were conferred on the greater princes in 1156, 1168
and 1180 enabling them, as intermediate authorities, to share in the
reconstitution of the hierarchy of government. The precondition of
this policy was loyal acceptance of feudal bonds on the part of the
princes; but provided the latter accepted the place assigned them in
the scheme of government, Frederick was content to exercise, beyond the bounds of his immediate demesnes, a feudal suzerainty

[1] According to Bishop Otto of Freising (*Gesta Friderici*, ed. Waitz and Simson, 1912,
p. 240) it was calculated in 1158 that a resumption of the usurped prerogatives of the crown
in Italy would bring in a revenue of approximately 30,000 talents annually. At the end of
last century Lamprecht (*Deutsche Geschichte* III, 134) calculated that this sum was the equivalent of 15,500,000 marks. Its present value may be set at approximately £1,500,000 per
annum, its purchasing capacity at more than ten times that sum.

such as that exercised in France by his contemporaries, Louis VII and Philip Augustus. There is evidence that Frederick was alive to the methods and policy of the Anglo-Norman and Capetian dynasties; and it is not too much to say that he set out to build in Germany a feudal monarchy such as already existed in France and England. The civil war and turmoil between 1076 and 1152 had given Germany, for better or worse, a feudal society: Frederick sought to direct the forces of feudalism into constructive channels and to organize German feudal society into a feudal state, culminating in a strong feudal kingship.

The success which attended Frederick's policy was remarkable. It is true that his attempt to introduce direct royal government into Lombardy was a failure, involving him in a bitter and protracted struggle with the Lombard communes and the papacy; but what he strove in vain to enforce in Lombardy in the earlier years of his reign, he achieved without difficulty in Tuscany and central Italy after the Peace of Venice (1177) and the Peace of Constance (1183). From 1177 onwards Frederick's efforts in Italy were concentrated on the extension of direct imperial administration throughout Tuscany and the central provinces; annual hearth-taxes were introduced, the country was divided into uniform administrative districts, and the administration was placed in the hands of a dependable bureaucracy. Geographically, this government was very different from that which Frederick had envisaged at the beginning of his reign; Tuscany and central Italy were the basis, not Lombardy, and instead of direct bureaucratic rule in the north his relations with the Lombard communes were governed by feudal principles. But despite the shift in the geographical balance, the main principles of government remained the same; the foundation was still a solidly administered royal territory, and outside that territory a federation held together by feudal bonds and by a balance of groups and interests which left the emperor, at the head, in ultimate control. This policy, which in Italy opened up new revenues and added on a large scale to the resources of the monarchy, was also the keynote of Frederick's government in Germany. Here also the resources of the monarchy were systematically developed. Under the year 1169 the chroniclers tell us of widespread acquisitions of properties by the crown; and it is clear that from about this date Frederick paid great attention to the consolidation of his territorial power in Swabia and to its extension through Franconia eastwards to the Bohemian Forest and north-wards into Saxony. Thus the king, whose material resources in 1152 had been inferior to those of many of the princes, gradually raised himself into a position of predominance. This predominance was assured in 1180 by the fall of Henry the Lion, the Welf duke of Saxony and Bavaria. Confident in his mighty territorial position in north Germany, the latter had grasped the opportunity, during Frederick's long struggle with the Lombard communes and the church, to challenge the monarchy and assert his own independence; but the events of 1180 showed that he had misjudged the situation, and that Frederick's reliance on the bonds of feudalism was not mis-placed. Tried and condemned by feudal law as a contumacious vassal, Henry was deprived of his fiefs, which reverted to the crown. The fall of Henry the Lion thus gave Frederick an unparalleled opportunity to reshape the political geography of Germany to the advantage of the monarchy. Saxony was divided into two duchies, Westphalia and Anhalt, and Styria was separated from Bavaria. In north and south the great Welf territorial *bloc* was split up, and in place of one overmighty vassal the king was left with a number of smaller princes, over whom he could more easily exercise effective control. Politically the events of 1180 were an outstanding success for the monarchy, and at the Diet of Mainz in 1184 Frederick appeared at the height of his power: it was, says the chronicler, 'so famous and celebrated a court that no other court can be compared with it'.

Contrasted with the precarious position under Frederick's prede-cessor, Conrad III, the progress achieved between 1152 and 1184 was astounding. It is true that in many parts of his empire Frederick's authority was only indirect; but the same was true at that date of Capetian France, and comparison with France should prevent our under-estimating the measure of Frederick's achievement. In both countries feudal overlordship, resolutely maintained, offered the prospect, with the gradual extension of the direct sphere of royal control, of national unity. But after Frederick's death in 1190, the divergence of French and German development was rapid. In France, the Capetians, maintaining hereditary succession and con-tinuity of policy, gradually extended direct royal administration over the feudal provinces, beginning with Normandy in 1204; in Germany, on the contrary, there began the large-scale diversion of

royal energies to Italy, accompanied by disputed successions, changes
in dynasty, and their attendant evils. Frederick's son, Henry VI
(1190-1197), who had married the heiress of Sicily in 1186, was not
indifferent to Germany; he spent much effort on the extension of the
royal demesnes and introduced a project of hereditary monarchy
which, if carried out, would have remedied one of the most serious
ills of the German constitution. But when, on the death without
direct heirs of William II, the last Norman king of Sicily, Henry laid
claim in his wife's name to the Sicilian succession, and established
himself in power by force of arms, he fatally compromised his
position by involving himself, his dynasty and Germany in the complications of Mediterranean politics. It has rightly been maintained
that Henry VI's conquest of Sicily in 1194 was a momentous turning-
point, perhaps the decisive turning-point, in German history.[1]
Henry himself quickly succumbed to the allurements which Sicily
held out, to the prospect of grandiose projects in the Mediterranean.
His preparations for an attack on the Byzantine empire, his crusade
and the suzerainty he established over the kings of Cyprus and
Armenia were all in Norman, not in German tradition, and be-
tokened a squandering of German blood and treasure on objects
which offered no lasting benefit to Germany. His early death in
1197, leaving only a two-year-old child as heir and thus opening the
way for a disputed succession, was connected with his preparations
for leading an army to Palestine. But most important of all, his
seizure of Sicily roused the implacable hostility of the papacy. The
union of Sicily and the empire threatened to crush the papacy in
Rome between the upper and nether millstones; it raised the spectre
of encirclement, and created a position which no pope who prized
his independence could long accept. Thus once again through the
Sicilian entanglement the papacy was drawn into German politics;
and once again, as in the days of Gregory VII, papal support
rallied the German factions and weighed the balance against the
monarchy.

On Henry VI's premature death in 1197 the evil consequences of
the Sicilian entanglement were immediately revealed. Determined

---

[1] The significance of the connexion of Germany and Sicily, the so-called *unio regni ad
imperium*, as a turning-point in German history, is still not always fully appreciated; it was con-
vincingly demonstrated many years ago by Julius Ficker in a famous essay of great historical
importance, *Das deutsche Kaiserreich in seinen universalen und nationalen Beziehungen* (1862),
pp. 99, 103 sq., 117.

to destroy the threat to papal independence, Innocent III (1198-1216), without weighing the consequences for Germany, used all his influence to secure a change of dynasty and thereby unleashed a civil war which undid much, if not all, that Frederick I had achieved. The majority of German princes, true to Hohenstaufen traditions, elected Philip of Swabia, the brother of Henry VI; but a small faction supported by the pope elected Otto of Brunswick, the son of Henry the Lion. The outcome of this double election was civil war. Without external support Otto's prospects were poor, and the unrest might soon have subsided; but now a new factor intervened. England and France, at war with each other and each anxious to secure German support, lent their backing to the rival candidates, fomenting German discords for their own purposes. Thus through foreign intervention the civil war was prolonged from 1198 to 1208, throwing Germany into a state of anarchy comparable with the worst phases of Henry IV's reign; and only Philip of Swabia's death brought it to an end. But no sooner was Otto of Brunswick secure on the throne than he showed that he had no intention of throwing over the policy of Henry VI; in 1209 he appeared in Italy and in 1210 began a campaign to reconquer Sicily. Thus all Innocent's plans seemed doomed to failure, and in despair he turned to the only candidate who had any hope of securing adequate support against Otto — namely, Henry VI's son, the young Frederick. In November 1210 Otto was excommunicated, and in 1212 Frederick with the pope's blessing made his way northwards to Germany. In Swabia, the hereditary land of his dynasty, he was well received; but his greatest asset was the backing of the king of France, who furnished him with funds to buy support. Otto, on the other hand, relied on England, and it is typical of the change which had come over German affairs since 1198 that the decisive factor in the contest between Otto and Frederick was the course of the Anglo-French war. In 1214 at Bouvines, a hamlet between Lille and Tournai, Philip Augustus of France inflicted a crushing defeat on Otto. After Bouvines Otto's position crumbled. There was no hope of support from the English king who was crippled by the unrest in England which led to Magna Carta, and Otto's adherents in Germany hastened to come to terms with Frederick. The latter received from the French king the imperial insignia which Otto had left lying on the field of battle, and was solemnly crowned in Aachen cathedral in 1215.

c

Such were the beginnings of the reign of Frederick II (1212-1250). The civil wars had given rein to the centrifugal tendencies of feudalism; once again the resources of the monarchy were plundered and wasted, and Frederick, no less than Otto and Philip before him, made extensive grants and concessions between 1212 and 1215 in order to secure adherents. Anglo-French intervention was a new and ominous factor, setting an evil precedent for the future; and Frederick II himself succeeded to the throne not at the will of the German people, or even of the German princes, but in pursuance of papal interests and with the help of French arms. It was an evil day for Germany when Innocent III summoned him to champion the papal cause against Otto IV. Frederick has been depicted as one of the great German emperors;[1] but in spite of the German blood flowing in his veins, he was by birth and upbringing a Sicilian, and his policy was the policy of a Sicilian king. Throughout Frederick II's reign Sicily and Italy came first; for the first time, and on a grand scale, the Italian elements in imperial government were developed at the expense of the German. And when in the end Frederick's plans for Italy, thwarted by the papacy and the Lombard cities, failed to materialize, Germany was pulled down in the ruin. Yet it was not the failure of Frederick's policy, so much as that policy itself, that was fatal for Germany's future. In spite of the political setbacks between 1198 and 1215, German social development, stimulated by the achievements of Frederick I, had gone ahead by leaps and bounds: German colonists were streaming east, new towns were springing up, chivalry was at its height, the German language in the hands of Wolfram von Eschenbach and Walther von der Vogelweide was becoming the vehicle of poetry and of a common German civilization, and German architecture was on the threshold of its greatest achievements at Cologne and Bamberg and Naumburg. But Frederick II, a child of the south, engrossed in Italy, turned his back on the opportunities which these developments offered to a German king conscious of his German heritage. Instead of taking the government of Germany in hand with a view to restoring the position of the monarchy after its decline between 1198 and 1215 — as Frederick I restored it after the upheavals of 1076-1152 — he left Germany to the

---

[1] This tendency is particularly marked in E. Kantorowicz's romantic biography, *Frederick the Second* (Engl. trans., 1931), but it is fair to say that the majority of historians have rejected his colourful phantasies; cf. the trenchant criticism by Brackmann, *Hist. Zeitschrift*, CXL (1929), and Hampe, *Hist. Zeitschrift*, CXLVI (1932).

princes and consumed his energies in the contest with the papacy which any essentially Italian policy involved.

The result of Frederick's reign was, therefore, a major advance in the power of the princes. Under him they became the effective rulers of Germany. Frederick counted no price too high to pay to secure the acquiescence of the princes in his Italian policy; and the concessions he made in his two famous privileges, the *Confoederatio cum principibus ecclesiasticis* of 1220 and the *Statutum in favorem principum* of 1232, were milestones along the road to territorial sovereignty. These concessions, covering courts and jurisdictions, the right to build castles and to levy new taxes, coinage and control over the cities within the boundaries of the growing principalities, cut away the ground from under the feet of the monarchy. They also created an ever-widening divergence of interests between the crown and the princes. Frederick I had found the means of bringing the principalities into harmony with the interests of the monarchy; and down to the thirteenth century their development had taken place under the crown within the framework of German unity, while the monarchy had retained sufficient independent power of its own to hold the princes in check. Under Frederick II the forces of unity withered. His continued absence from Germany dissociated the princes from the imperial government; personal association with the king, participation in the business of government, in legislation and in judgment, the traditional duty of attendance and service at court, all these ceased, and therewith ceased the main concrete demonstrations of the existence of a unity towering above the princes, of an organization of which the princes were only members. Frederick II's neglect of his royal duties turned the princes into egoists: dissociated from the empire, which was now Italian or Sicilian rather than German in character, they devoted their main energies to rounding-off and building-up their territorial power, and regarded imperial affairs mainly as an opportunity for wringing further concessions from the crown. When conflict broke out between Frederick and the papacy, they took up an independent position between the two parties, extorting payment from both for their services and support. Hence the real victor in the contest between Frederick and the papacy, which broke out in 1239, was the estate of princes. To secure support Frederick and his son, Conrad, alienated the hereditary demesnes of the crown, and in this way the monarchy lost the independent territorial basis which alone could make the king's prerogatives a reality; without a strongly organized territory and adequate material resources the monarchy was unable to maintain its authority, and the result was atrophy, loss and powerlessness.

Between 1212, when Frederick first appeared in Germany, and 1250 the old foundations of royal government perished, and the long interregnum which followed Frederick's death in 1250 only consolidated the changes in the distribution of political power in which his German policy resulted. The consequence of his neglect was to throw Germany back, to check its development by comparison with England and France. The functions carried out elsewhere by a strong monarchy — the protection (for example) of public peace and the suppression of crime — were in Germany either carried out by private associations within limited areas for limited purposes, or were not carried out at all. The centralized machinery of law enforcement, which in England was in formation in the days of Henry II, had no parallel in Germany, and it was only later and haltingly that a similar organization was formed in the principalities. In 1250 the whole organization of German government, which had been ahead of the rest of Europe at the close of the eleventh century, was extraordinarily retrograde; and for this the growing tendency to rely on Italian resources must be blamed. Frederick II made little attempt to develop his resources in Germany; at the very time when he was reorganizing Sicilian and Italian government on modern, bureaucratic lines, he allowed the organs of German government to atrophy, and what development there was towards more modern forms of administration was due to the princes and worked for the benefit of the princes. The result was to place political power in the princes' hands. It has been calculated that the demesnes of the crown at the end of the Hohenstaufen period amounted in the aggregate to the equivalent of only three-quarters of the margraviate of Brandenburg; but they were scattered fragments and provided a weak basis for political power which could not compare with the resources of the greater princes. Hence the allegiance of the princes was based no longer on respect for a monarch who was powerful enough to make his authority felt, but rather on compromises, capitulations and promises. After 1250 the electoral principle, combated until the very end of Hohenstaufen times, became a tenet of constitutional law, and with the establishment of elective monarchy the king became a puppet of the princes. Within a few years the destinies of Germany fell into the hands of the electoral college, and the electoral college represented the interests of the principalities. Thus the defection of the monarchy, the abdication by Frederick II of his German tasks, involved disruption. The extraordinary vigour which was developed precisely at this time by German town life and commerce, the rich bloom of German civilization, were diverted and wasted in narrow provincial channels. Without the unity provided by the crown, the principalities of north and east Germany went their own way, ful-filling a destiny which was provincial rather than national. Germany was condemned for centuries to decentralization and disunion and to the evils which went with decentralization and the unchecked conflicts of competing interests.

§ 6. *The Victory of the Princes* (1250-1356)

Frederick II's reign ended in bankruptcy. From the moment of his death it was clear that he had left no system capable of standing fast once his personality was removed. Throughout the empire every unwholesome development of the preceding fifty years was im-mediately accentuated. Sicily rose in rebellion; in Italy the local powers assumed control and laid the foundations of the *signorie* or tyrannies, which soon became the dominant factor in Italian politics; in Germany the long Interregnum between 1250 and 1272 enabled the princes to consolidate all they had won during Frederick's reign. The links between Germany and Italy were shattered, and the con-stituent parts of the empire went their own way in independent development, while in Germany itself the monarchy underwent an eclipse. Frederick's son, Conrad IV, failed to secure any adherents of importance, and for the first time in German history there was no solid body of support, among either princes or bishops, for the legitimate dynasty. The different kings put up by contending fac-tions were either foreign nominees, like Richard of Cornwall or Alfonso of Castile, who never set foot in Germany, or petty counts like William of Holland, who were not powerful enough to establish effective government. Except for the towns, which the lack of royal authority left a prey to princely ambitions, there was no politically effective party seriously interested in a restoration of stable govern-ment. The princes, intent on despoiling what remained of the royal estates, had no desire for a strong king, who might pursue a policy of recuperation; with the election of William of Holland (1247-1256), the first German king who was not of princely rank, the ominous tendency emerged to select weak rulers, incapable for lack of territorial power of checking the territorial ambitions of the princes.

The Interregnum of 1250-1272, enabling the princes to consolidate their position at the expense of the monarchy, and weakening the forces of law and order, was a serious setback to German national development. The collapse of the Hohenstaufen empire, on the other hand, although it registered a decline of Germany's standing in Europe, was far from being an unmitigated loss. The empire and imperial traditions had once been a bond of unity, which had contributed to the unification of the German people; but that time was past, and no good had come of the subordination of Germany to Italy which was the mark of Frederick II's reign. Moreover, mediaeval means of government were inadequate for rule over wide areas, and it is scarcely to be doubted that something of the backwardness of German government was due to the dissipation of effort which imperial policy required. In the rest of Europe the end of the thirteenth century saw the rise under strong kings of national states, pursuing national policies; this was the case in France under Philip the Fair (1285-1314), in England under Edward I (1272-1307), and in Spain under Peter III of Aragon (1276-1285). The collapse of the Hohenstaufen empire opened up similar prospects for Germany. In spite of the strengthening of the princes between 1250 and 1272 there was still the possibility, once the connexion with Italy was severed, of the formation of a national monarchy under a national dynasty; and the interest of the period 1272-1356 in German history lies in the struggle to reshape German political organization and bring it into the current of national development which was so strong in Europe at the end of the thirteenth century. Between 1272 and 1356 two conflicting tendencies were at play in Germany, the one leading to the conquest of sovereignty by the princes, the other working for a reconstitution of royal authority on new foundations; and until these conflicting tendencies had, under the pressure of political events, crystallized out, Germany's future hung in the balance.

After the accession of Rudolf of Habsburg (1273-1291), whose election put an end to the Interregnum, the prospects of a revival of the monarchy under the Habsburg dynasty were good. Rudolf and his son Albrecht (1298-1308) strove hard to lay the foundations for an effective national kingship, concentrating their efforts on building up the Habsburg territories; for after 1250 the king no longer had any substantial authority as king, and could only rule Germany effectively if he were the greatest of the princes. In this respect good progress was achieved.[1] Albrecht had inherited considerable territories from his father in south Germany, in Alsace, the Black Forest and Switzerland, and to these Austria and Styria were added in 1278. When, supported by the towns, he broke the opposition of the electoral princes in 1301 and 1302, and then set out to win Bohemia, Meissen and Thuringia, success seemed near at hand. Habsburg policy was to exchange the empty imperial title for hereditary succession in Germany, to transform Germany into an hereditary monarchy and, having established continuity of policy and abrogated the rights of the electors, gradually to extend the sphere of royal power and break down the resistance of the princes. It was a statesmanlike plan; but three factors prevented its realization. The first was the opposition within Germany, led by the electoral princes of the Rhinelands, who feared for the loss of their prerogatives, and therefore resisted all attempts to introduce hereditary succession; after Rudolf's death, they manoeuvred the election of a petty Rhenish count, Adolf of Nassau (1292-1298), after Albrecht's death they secured the rejection of his son and the transfer of the crown to Henry of Luxemburg (1308-1313). The second factor, more sinister, was foreign intervention, particularly the intervention of France whose kings strove to keep Germany weak and politically divided in order the more easily to annex German territories in the west; France allied with German factions and fomented German resistance to Adolf of Nassau and Albrecht of Habsburg, and French intervention was the prime cause of the failure of Ludwig of Bavaria (1314-1347) to establish a stable monarchy. Finally, the establishment of a national monarchy in Germany was hindered by the persistence, long after Hohenstaufen times, of imperial traditions. At a time when French political thought was busy laying the foundations of the nation-state, German political theory, as represented by Jordan of

[1] G. von Below, *Vom Mittelalter zur Neuzeit* (1924), 31, described the work of Rudolf of Habsburg by saying that 'he was on the way to subduing the territorial states through the territorial state' — i.e. by making the ruling dynasty the strongest territorial power in Germany.

Osnabrück or Englebert of Admont, was still rooted to the empire; and this attitude was not confined to theory. Henry VII (1308-1313) sought for a brief moment to revive the Italian policy of the Hohen-staufen, and other kings, for example Adolf of Nassau, devoted much energy to the defence of Burgundy against France. Thus German policy vacillated, from reign to reign, between two poles: either to save what could be saved of the imperial connexion and of the imperial territories, or to cut away from the imperial tradition and concentrate on national development. But the persistence of the trappings of imperialism had other more direct consequences. It kept alive papal fears of renewed German intervention in Italy, and gave the pope a valid excuse for interference in German affairs. Since the German king was still potentially emperor, the pope claimed the right to scrutinize all elections and to confirm or reject any candidate for the throne. Thus the fate of Germany was in some measure in the hands of the pope at a time when the papacy, in captivity at Avignon, was in the hands of France; and the interven-tion of popes such as John XXII (1316-1334) was an important factor in preventing the recovery of the German monarchy. When we condemn the evil consequences of German particularism and princely egoism, we must not forget the effects of French and papal inter-ference in promoting discord and checking the forces making for a healthy development of the German constitution. It was largely through the action of those European powers whose interests would have suffered through the consolidation of Germany under effective monarchical government that the principle of elective monarchy was established and Germany passed under the control of the estate of princes.

The turning-point was the long reign of Ludwig of Bavaria (1314-1347). His defeat of Frederick of Austria in 1322 put an end once and for all to the Habsburg scheme of an hereditary German kingship; but he himself, in face of French and papal opposition, was unable to carry through similar plans. Philip VI of France raised the house of Luxemburg, now in possession of Bohemia, in opposition against him, and exerted pressure on Pope Benedict XII to prevent a recon-ciliation with the papacy. The result was a remarkable recrudescence of German national feeling. Revolting against Franco-papal pres-sure, the estates of the realm at the Diet of Rhens (1338) rejected papal interference and proclaimed the independence of the German

monarchy.[1] In happier circumstances this movement might have
provided a decisive stimulus to national solidarity behind the crown;
but this was not to be. Franco-papal intrigue went on; Ludwig in
vain tried to appease the new pope, Clement VI (1342-1352), but no
concession was enough; and the princes, beginning to feel that only
the king's person stood between Germany and peace, wavered in
their support. In 1346 Charles of Luxemburg was elected in Ludwig's place, and after the latter's death in 1347, he quickly won
universal recognition as legitimate king. With the accession of
Charles IV (1346-1378) the issue which had divided Germany since
1272 was decided. Faced by chaotic conditions in every corner of the
realm, the legacy of the previous reign, Charles IV had no mind to
continue the struggle waged by his predecessor. Realizing that the
intervention of the papacy in the election and confirmation of the
German king was a prime cause of dissension in Germany, his first
object was to break the bonds by which Germany had so long been
subjected to the dictates of papal policy; and this he achieved on lines
already foreshadowed in 1338. But in order to secure unity against
the pope, he had to make far-reaching concessions to the German
princes, sanctioning the rights they had amassed and according
solemn legal recognition of their privileges. Hence the exclusion of
papal influence, which took place in 1356, instead of strengthening
the internal position of the monarchy, resulted in the consolidation
of the rights of the electors and of princes, such as the duke of
Austria, who without being electors had already established their
territorial power.

The instrument in which these fundamental constitutional changes
were laid down was the famous Golden Bull of 1356. To shake free
from the papacy, Charles IV deliberately based the monarchy on the
princes. The rights and functions of the electors were clearly defined,
and to prevent disputed elections, which might reopen the door to
papal interference, precise rules were drawn up to prevent the
division of the electorates and therewith the multiplication of elec-

---

[1] The protest of Rhens was re-enacted by Ludwig as a law of the empire. This law, the
constitution *Licet iuris* (1338), after denouncing those who 'wrongfully assert that the emperor
derives his position and authority from the pope' — which is described as a false and dangerous
doctrine, the work of the 'ancient enemy of mankind, attempting to stir up strife and discord
and bring about confusion and dissension' — goes on to declare 'that the emperor holds his
authority and position from God alone . . . and has full power to administer the laws and to
perform all the functions of emperor, without the approval, confirmation, authorization or
consent of the pope or any other person'.

toral votes. In this way the electorates were established as fixed elements in German political life; kings might change, the crown pass from dynasty to dynasty, but the electors remained, the enduring factors which no king henceforward could displace without tearing up the constitution. The result of the Golden Bull was, therefore, to establish a fixed constitutional relationship between the emperor and the princes, which was to endure with only unimportant modifications until the dissolution of the Holy Roman empire in 1806. At the same time the confirmation of rights of coinage and the monopoly of gold, silver and other metals within their territories gave the electors a semi-regal position, which was enhanced by the application to offences against their persons of the penalties of *lèse-majesté*. The seven electors were (the Golden Bull proclaimed) the seven luminaries, the *candelabra lucentia* illuminating the realm; they were 'the solid foundations and immovable pillars of the empire'.

The Golden Bull thus established, after a period of instability and conflicting tendencies extending from 1250 to 1356, a federal framework for German political life, in which the princes were the dominant power. It has sometimes been asked whether this was an innovation or merely a confirmation of the *status quo*. The answer is that the Golden Bull sanctioned developments which rested on long precedent, but which until that date had never definitely secured acceptance as a recognized scheme of government. It marked the cessation of the attempt to maintain an independent position for the monarchy. After 1356 the principalities were firmly anchored in the constitution, and there could be no attempt to revive the monarchy at the expense of the princes. The crown was henceforward a nullity and German unity a mere façade. Charles IV himself in the Golden Bull emphasized 'the variety of customs, ways of life and language of the various nations' included in the empire, and insisted on the need for 'laws and a method of government that take all this variety into account'. He may have been right; but the result was that Germany advanced towards modern times divided and disunited, under the control of princes whose dynastic interests were no substitute for a German policy and whose rivalries prevented the maintenance of German interests. After 1356 German energies, which as late as 1338 had still responded to the national call, were diverted from the Reich to the principalities; Germany faded into the background and the German territorial states advanced to the front of the stage.

CHAPTER II

THE TRANSITION TO MODERN TIMES
(1356-1519)

§ 7. *The Mediaeval Legacy*

THE development sketched in the preceding chapter is the background to modern German history. It shows us how Germany, which began in the ninth century on a par with the other states springing from the soil of the Carolingian empire, and was for long in advance in its evolution, gradually fell behind France in political development. It is true that from the beginning German history is differentiated in certain respects from that of France;[1] but the true cause of the aberrations of German evolution, the weakening of the monarchy and the growth of particularism, lies not in initial differences but in the factors emerging, from the end of the eleventh century, in the course of historical development. We may perhaps attach importance to the early limitations of feudalism in Germany, to the weakness of the bonds of vassalage, which elsewhere proved a source of social cohesion;[2] for the strong sense of independence and 'liberty' and the insistence on its inherited 'rights' which still characterized the German nobility in the eleventh century were without doubt one reason why we find it allying with the church against the monarchy at a time when elsewhere (for example, in England) the monarchy could rely on the support of the baronage against papal pretensions. For this reason it has been said, not without justification, that 'papal intervention never achieved any success worth mention except as the ally of German faction'.[3] But it is scarcely less true to say that the success of German factions was the result of their alliances with the papacy. Fundamentally it was the attack on two fronts, the alliance between the German opposition and the papacy, seconded at a later stage by France, that

---

[1] Cf. above, pp. 2, 5-6.

[2] The contrast in this respect between France and Germany was effectively drawn by L. Reynaud, *Les origines de l'influence française en Allemagne* (1913), 153 sqq., and by M. Bloch, *La société féodale*, I (1939), 276 sqq., 409 sqq.

[3] Such was the view of E. Rosenstock, *Königshaus und Stämme in Deutschland zwischen 911 und 1250* (1914), 222.

defeated all attempts by the Salian and Hohenstaufen dynasties and by their successors after the Interregnum, to set German government on a durable foundation.

A second factor was the imperial question. Perhaps no question of mediaeval history has caused greater controversy in recent times than the attempt to evaluate the effects of the imperial connexion on German history, to draw up a balance-sheet for or against the imperial policy of the rulers of mediaeval Germany. There can be no question here of attempting to resume, still less to pursue further, this great controversial issue.[1] The answer is certainly not so simple as many historians appear to have thought; there are many imponderable factors which leave wide scope for divergence of view. But two points already noticed in the text should be emphasized: first, that the 'revival' of the empire by Otto I in 962 was not (as is sometimes suggested) the result of a 'blind urge to conquer', but rather an integral part of the Carolingian tradition on which Ottonian government was based; and secondly, that there is no evidence down to the death of Frederick I in 1190 that German interests and Germany's welfare were sacrificed to Italy. To speak, as one historian has done,[2] of 'Frederick I's caesaristic madness', of infatuation 'with the grandiose idea of mediaeval imperialism', is to import prejudice into history. On the other hand, there is no doubt about the disastrous consequences of the connexion forged between Germany and Sicily in 1194. But it is scarcely justifiable to treat the developments which occurred after the union of Germany and Sicily as the inevitable consequences of German imperialism as it had developed since 962. It was not inevitable that Frederick II should neglect Germany and treat his German inheritance with indifference; and his attitude to the

[1] The controversy, begun in 1859 as a sequel to the publication in 1855 of the first volume of Giesebrecht's monumental *Geschichte der deutschen Kaiserzeit*, was in origin less historical than political, and reflected the views of the two main parties of the period, the 'Kleindeutschen' (who advocated a Prussian solution of the problems of the day, to the exclusion of Austria) and the 'Grossdeutschen' (who hoped for a German empire including Austria and Prussia). Sybel, a Prussian, attacked Giesebrecht's favourable verdict on the mediaeval empire; he, in his turn, was attacked by Ficker. The discussion was for long marred by the political prejudices it reflected; but in the present century a more dispassionate and scientific spirit resulted in a better understanding of the problems. Unfortunately this later work has largely been ignored in England, where there has been no attempt since the works of Bryce (revised ed., 1907) and Fisher (1908), neither of which is any longer satisfactory, to reassess and rewrite the history of the empire in the light of modern knowledge. In German a convenient summary was provided in 1934 by F. Schneider, *Neuere Anschauungen der deutschen Historiker zur Beurteilung der deutschen Kaiserpolitik des Mittelalters* (2nd ed., 1936).

[2] J. W. Thompson, *Feudal Germany* (1928), 275, 277.

empire, far from being the culmination of mediaeval imperialism, marked an abrupt breach with the past. He abandoned the traditions on which his German predecessors had built, and substituted a Mediterranean tradition compounded of Norman lust for conquest, Italian tyranny and oriental cynicism, in which the dawn of a new — and scarcely better — age was heralded; he sacrificed Germany to an imperialism which was not German, but Sicilian or Italian. On the other hand, there was one way in which, long before the thirteenth century, the connexion with Italy seriously affected the course of German affairs; and this was in aggravating relations with the papacy. It was no accident that the immediate cause of the conflict between Henry IV and Gregory VII was the question of the appointment of the archbishop of Milan; and the unrelenting nature of the conflict which followed was due in large degree to the fact that control over the Italian church was at issue. The papacy found little difficulty in compromising with the kings of England and France over the control of episcopal appointments; but it could not compromise with the German ruler without injuring its own position in Italy. Hence the imperial connexion was at the back of the conflict with the papacy which, as we have seen, fatally impeded the smooth development of German government; in the same way the fact that the German king was also emperor-designate gave the pope a pretext to intervene in German affairs which Innocent III used with disastrous effects.

It is probable that none of these factors alone would have been sufficient to weigh the balance against the monarchy; what was decisive was their combination. The results, as Germany made the transition from mediaeval to modern times, were threefold. The first was that German political development, checked by repeated conflicts, was retarded. Secondly, the development of a modern system of government, when it did begin, was transferred from the whole to the parts, from the nation to the principalities; Germany was deprived of the benefit of centralized control and guidance, which did so much to preserve the continuity of English history, and even of effective central institutions. Instead, the development of the institutions which in France and England led to the sovereign state, of taxation and legislation, of assemblies and government departments, took place in the principalities. But even here it was slow and halting, because there was no direct transfer of existing rights and functions from the empire to the territorial states after 1250. The old idea that the rise of the principalities was due to the usurpation by the princes of existing rights of government accounts for only a very small part of their powers, which in reality were built, slowly and laboriously, on new foundations, fulfilling functions which no monarchy in the early middle ages had sought to perform. But there was one function, accomplished by the imperial government down to 1250, which the principalities could not fulfil; and that was the defence of the frontiers. One of the main factors differentiating Germany on the threshold of modern times from Germany in the middle ages, was weakness on all its frontiers, and particularly in the west. This, the third factor in the transitional period when power passed from the empire to the principalities, was the corollary of internal territorial divisions, which made it easy for foreign powers to play off one prince against another and prevented united resistance to the aggressor. And yet even at this time of growing fragmentation, when the princes were firmly established in the saddle, the sense of German unity, inculcated during the past three centuries, remained strong. Switzerland, strongly pro-imperial out of antipathy to the house of Austria, was still within the empire and remained there until 1495, and only the Netherlands, involved in the ephemeral Burgundian state, tended to break away.[1] Of all the work of the early German emperors, from Otto I to the Hohenstaufen, perhaps none was more important than their success in establishing a sense of German unity which persisted even when the empire had ceased to be a political reality; herein we may rightly see the most enduring achievement of the old German monarchy, and the one with most weighty consequences in modern times.

The legacy of the middle ages was, therefore, on one side, the territorial principalities and, on the other, the principle of unity created by the empire; in other words, the tendency to dispersal and fragmentation, and the tendency to cohesion. These antithetical factors lie at the roots of modern German history, which is, in one respect, little more than a commentary on their conflict. In the later middle ages, approximately between 1356 and 1519, a second antithesis emerges, equally fundamental for German history in modern times. This is the antithesis between representative assemblies, the germ of popular government, and the unfettered power of the

[1] Cf. below, p. 57.

princes. It needs no proof that the two sets of factors were closely interdependent. For the princes the territorial system was a means of assuring their power, and so there is a close association between the consolidation of the principalities and the rise of princely absolutism, while slowly — and, indeed, haltingly — the forces of unity and democracy draw together. Equally the interdependence of internal and external unity needs no demonstration. So long as Germany was divided internally, it was a prey to foreign powers, and so there arises an intimate connexion between foreign affairs and the maintenance of the independent German territorial states. The interference of aggressive powers seeking to preserve or create German disunity is a major factor throughout modern German history, which has not ceased to count even to-day. But its origins take us back to the Interregnum of 1250-1272; it was then, and in the succeeding century, that the traditions were formed which, in the wars to which they have given rise, have wearied and wasted successive generations of Europeans.

§ 8. *The Problem of the Western Frontier*

When Philip Augustus sent Frederick II the damaged imperial insignia from the battlefield of Bouvines in 1214,[1] it was a truly symbolic gesture. 'From this time forward', a chronicler wrote, 'the fame of the Germans sank ever lower among foreigners.' The generation 1198-1215 witnessed a radical shift in the European balance of power to the detriment of Germany, and the first steps towards French hegemony in Europe. But it was only after the extinction of the Hohenstaufen dynasty in 1268 that French hegemony was established, under the successors of St. Louis, Philip III (1270-1285) and Philip IV (1285-1314). After 1250 the scramble for a share in the spoils which had fallen from the hands of the Hohenstaufen, the division of the corpse of the Hohenstaufen empire, became a dominating theme in European politics, in which all the major powers were implicated in one degree or another. Foremost of all was France, which set out in particular to absorb the imperial territories of Burgundy. But there was no natural division between the old kingdom of Burgundy, which had been part of the empire since

[1] Cf. above, p. 23.

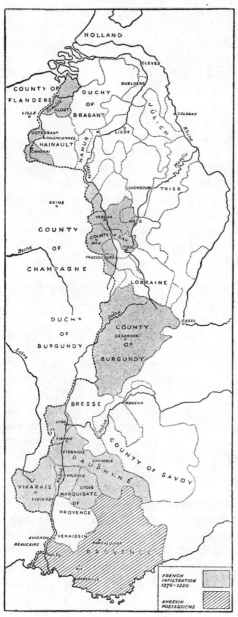

The Franco-German and Franco-imperial frontiers, c. 1270-1350.

1034, and the German lands to the north; and under Philip IV French pressure was gradually extended until it developed into a consistent attack along the whole line of Germany's western frontier.

The importance of the period beginning with the accession of Philip III in 1270 is that it established the enduring framework of Franco-German relations. French policy at this period can only be understood if it is examined in detail; for, although there were a number of plans for large-scale transfers of territory, these only exceptionally produced concrete results, and the essence of French policy was piecemeal encroachment, a niggling warfare of parchments and precedents, of litigation and blackmail, by which the French frontiers were advanced step by step into German territory. The first broad objective was the line of the rivers

Scheldt-Meuse-Saône-Rhône, all of which formed for part of their course the Franco-imperial frontier; but the beginning was intervention at single points, interference in local rivalries, the offer and often the imposition of French 'protection', or the issue of a summons to appear before a French official across the border, and it was only gradually that the single points of French penetration were linked together and a general advance inaugurated along the whole line. Under Philip III expansion was directed towards the rivers Meuse and Rhône; in the south Avignon, Lyons and the Vivarais were the scenes of French pressure, in the north the bishopric of Toul was brought under French protection in 1281. Under Philip IV it was extended to comprise also the areas west of Scheldt and Saône, and the most extensive gain was the establishment, in 1307, of effective French authority in the county of Burgundy (the *Freigrafschaft* or *Franche-Comté*). But more important for the future was French penetration into Lorraine, and the extension in 1299 of the French frontiers to the Meuse. The duke of Lorraine and the count of Bar were forced to do homage and service for part of their territories to the French king, and thenceforward there was a German Bar and a French Barrois, a German Lothringen and a French Lorraine. Down to the time of Richelieu, the parts of Bar west of the Meuse — the so-called *Barrois mouvant* — ceded to France in 1299 were a cornerstone of French policy and a stepping-stone for further French penetration into Lorraine.

The traditions of Philip IV received new impetus under Philip VI (1328-1350). In the north his objective was the territory of Cambrai, garrisoned in 1339 by French troops; in the south his main acquisition was the Delphinat or Dauphiné of Vienne which, following on the incorporation of Lyons and neighbouring territories under Philip IV, meant that France had won the lion's share of the old kingdom of Arles. The acquisition of the Dauphiné in 1349 was the last great French annexation of imperial territory in the middle ages; thereafter the reverses suffered in the Hundred Years War with England set a halt to French expansion, and gave Germany a temporary respite. At the same time the rise of Burgundy created an entirely new situation, with a formidable state interposed between France and Germany, encroaching on both. But between 1270 and 1350 the foundations of French policy on its eastern frontier had been laid; and Richelieu and Napoleon only needed to follow the

D

traditions created by Philip the Fair. Already in the fifteenth century, before the Burgundian menace had been overcome, these traditions were revived. In 1444 Charles VII entered Lorraine and summoned the cities between the Meuse and the Vosges to accept his authority, while another army advanced into Alsace; and in both cases the pretext was 'to reassert the rights of the kingdom of Gaul, which formerly extended to the Rhine', to enforce French sovereignty over cities and territories which, because they were situated on the left bank of the Rhine, 'ought by ancient right to appertain to the kings of France'.[1] The injury sustained by Germany in the west between 1270 and 1350 was, therefore, not confined to territorial losses, severe as these were; it lay also in the elaboration of a technique of French foreign policy which, having acquired the Scheldt-Meuse-Saône-Rhône frontier, could be used without modification as an instrument for obtaining the Rhine frontier and if necessary for encroachment beyond the Rhine. So long as Germany could be kept in the state of internal fragmentation to which it had been reduced by the collapse of central authority after 1250, there was no prospect of successful resistance to French aggression. Hence the middle ages left Germany faced by a double problem of great complexity: on the one hand, it was imperative to devise some form of unity which would enable Germany to resist French pressure, while on the other hand it was clear that the re-establishment of political unity could not be achieved without the elimination of French influence. This problem was scarcely tackled seriously before the nineteenth century; but its existence was one of the major factors conditioning German history in modern times, and it is here that we must seek the explanation of the particular type of unified state which Germany adopted in 1871.

§ 9. *German Eastern Expansion and Colonization*

While in the west the German frontiers were gradually yielding to French pressure, in the east a great wave of German colonization was carrying the frontiers of the Reich forward from the Elbe to the Vistula and along the shores of the Baltic to the Gulf of Finland. This colonizing movement, maintained for something over two centuries, from approximately 1125 to 1350, was one of the major

---

[1] Cf. A. Sorel, *L'Europe et la révolution française*, I (*Les moeurs politiques et les traditions*), 255-56.

factors differentiating modern from mediaeval Germany. It ushered in a new era of German history, changing not only the whole political balance but also the economic and social substructure of German life. It has been aptly described as 'the greatest deed of the German people during the middle ages'.[1] It gave for all time a new direction to German aspirations, a new outlet for German energies; it added to Germany an area equivalent in dimensions to two-thirds of its original territories. The Elbe, hitherto Germany's eastern frontier, henceforward ran through the heart of the land, taking the place of the Rhine as the centre of German life; Breslau replaced Magdeburg or Brandenburg as a frontier city.

There can be no question here of tracing, stage by stage, the course of German eastern expansion. Whereas in the west Germany came face to face with a neighbour united in the thirteenth century under a strong monarchy, along its eastern frontier it was confronted by a large number of small Slav tribes, divided among themselves, retrograde in political development and living in primitive economic conditions. In the earlier middle ages — particularly in the days of Boleslav III of Poland (1102-1139) — it had more than once appeared that a large Slav state was on the point of formation; but none of these attempts led to permanent results, not least because of the resistance of the smaller Slav peoples to Polish hegemony, which threatened their independence and the survival of their traditional way of life. There was no sense of Slav racial unity against the Germans; and both Pomerania and Brandenburg preferred, and deliberately chose, German domination to the 'hated overlordship' of Poland.[2] It was only in the latter part of the fourteenth and in the fifteenth centuries, after the main work of German colonization had been completed, that political antagonism became a serious factor on Germany's eastern frontiers. The rise of Hungary under Louis the Great (1342-1382), Bohemia under Charles IV (1346-1378), and Poland under Casimir the Great (1333-1376), transformed the situation. Poland, which had annexed the Russian kingdom of Galicia in 1340, became a great power after its union with Lithuania in 1386, and under Wladislav II (1386-1434) aspired to the leadership of eastern Europe. Already in 1308, after the extinction of the native Pomerel-

<hr/>

[1] K. Lamprecht, *Deutsche Geschichte*, III, 363: 'es ist die Grosstat unseres Volkes während des Mittelalters'.
[2] Cf. Thompson, *Feudal Germany*, 433, 446.

ian dynasty it had sought unsuccessfully to annex Pomerelia and thus to secure by conquest the port of Danzig and an outlet to the Baltic. After the defeat of the Teutonic Knights at Tannenberg in 1410, the Germans were thrown back on to the defensive, and in 1466 the peace of Thorn registered the decline of the Teutonic Order and established Polish sovereignty on the shores of the Baltic. Somewhat later the emergence of Russia as a great power under Ivan the Great (1462-1505) threatened the Order's hold in Livonia.

This reaction, which gathered strength in Poland and Bohemia in the last decades of the fourteenth century, set a definite term to German eastward expansion. Down to 1350, on the other hand, there was no fundamental opposition to the influx of German colonists. Princes such as Ottokar II of Bohemia (1253-1278) called in German knights and urban settlers on a large scale, and it should not be forgotten that it was the Polish duke of Masovia who summoned the Teutonic Order in 1226 to help him subdue the independent Prussians. But it would be a serious error to exaggerate the military element in the colonizing movement. From the tenth century onwards border warfare, bitter and bloody, had been endemic between the Saxons and the Slav tribes along the Elbe — Sorbs and Wends, Abotrites and Wagrians — and the prospect of conquest and of exploiting the conquered population played a large part in launching the movement of expansion in the twelfth century. But this early phase, culminating in the Wendish crusade of 1147, was of limited duration and importance. The object of princes such as Henry the Lion (1139-1195) was not colonization but the exaction of tribute; and the fall of Henry the Lion in 1180 brought this military and predatory phase to an end. After 1180 north Germany and the eastern shores of the Baltic passed for a generation under Danish hegemony, and when the German eastern movement was restarted, it was — apart from the conquest of Prussia by the Teutonic Knights between 1226 and 1283 — a movement not of warriors and princes, but of peasant settlers and traders. If Holstein and western Mecklenburg were mercilessly conquered by the sword, in Brandenburg, Pomerania and Silesia the sword gave way to the plough and German settlement took place without serious friction or bloodshed.

What gave German eastern expansion the character of a sweeping, irrevocable movement of peoples, changing for all time the ethnographical and political map of eastern Europe, was the ungrudging labour of thousands of peasants and urban settlers. This large-scale movement of population dates from 1210-1230, the period of Danish political predominance, and was the work as much of Slav as of German lords and princes. Urged on by the prospect of economic advantage, by the hope of profit from lands which had hitherto given no yield, all parties competed for the services of German settlers. It

The Germans in the Baltic (thirteenth and fourteenth centuries), showing the lands of the Teutonic Order.

was at this period that German emigrants entered eastern Mecklenburg and eastern Brandenburg, Pomerania, Silesia, northern Moravia and Poland. By the thirties of the thirteenth century they were across the new territory of the Teutonic knights on the lower Vistula, by Kulm and Thorn. Farther south, in Brandenburg, the line of the Oder was reached by 1240, and after 1242 the Neumark was formed east of the Oder with Frankfurt (founded in 1253) as a centre of communications, a crossing-place and an entry to the east. At Lebus, where the population was still predominantly Slav (it was the ancient land of the Leubuzzi), the native princes were so active in attracting colonists that between 1204 and 1239 they are reported to have recovered over 160,000 acres of waste or marshland. In Silesia the main phase of colonization occurred under Duke Henry I (1201-1238), a Slav prince with a German mother, who called in German settlers from the Elbe-Saale region. Meanwhile German settlers had sailed from Lübeck to Livonia, where the episcopal see of Riga was founded in 1186, and before the end of the twelfth century German merchants had warehouses as far afield as Novgorod, Pleskau and Smolensk. But the lack of a land route prevented peasant settlement in Livonia, and there was never any appreciable colonization, outside the towns, of lands bordering the Gulfs of Riga and Finland.

No overall figures of the numbers of German colonists can be given, but it has been calculated that in Silesia alone about 1200 villages were founded in the period 1200-1350, and that in a comparable period in East Prussia the knights and bishops established about 1400 rent-paying villages.[1] Taken together, these settlements would require a peasant population in the region of 300,000. Such figures, extended to cover the other centres of colonization, Mecklenburg and Holstein, Brandenburg and Pomerania, give the best idea of the magnitude of the task and the flow of population involved. What attracted settlers on such a scale was the prospect of favourable conditions, of a fixed tenure and legal security, and of personal freedom. East of the Elbe there were vast areas of virgin forest, marshlands which the natives were unable to dike and drain, and reserves of uncultivated waste, without competing for lands already under cultivation; and it was the achievement of the German colonists to win these wastes for culture, to plant villages in hundreds where previously humans had never trod, and to establish urban communities linking together the peasant settlements. Thus a sparsely populated land of negligible economic value was rendered productive. But in order to secure settlers to carry out this work, princes and landlords had to offer special concessions; and the primary inducement was exemption from the exasperating and obsolescent manorial burdens which hampered the peasants' initiative in the homeland. Unlike the bulk of the peasants in old west Germany, the colonists east of the Elbe had no work to do for their lords. Instead they received for moderate fixed rents holdings which were heritable and freely alienable. The settler in the east was not part of a manor, attached to a rigid manorial economy; and it was only in later centuries that developments set in leading to the depression of the peasantry and the growth of the aristocratic *Rittergut*.[2] In the period

---

[1] The statistics are given by H. Aubin in the *Cambridge Economic History*, I (1941), 396-97.
[2] Cf. below, p. 90-92.

of colonization the knight class in the east failed to secure that manorial control over rural economy and rural society, which was the main foundation of its power in the west. The knight's estate was generally small — often only the equivalent of a big peasant holding, rarely more than twice or four times that extent — and the knight himself was (in a famous phrase) 'the peasants' neighbour' rather than his lord; neither economically nor politically was he in control.

The freer economic conditions of the colonial east had two important consequences. In the first place, the advantages enjoyed by the German settlers were passed on to the native population, as it was gradually assimilated and Germanized; and the result was therefore a steady rise in the status of the labouring classes throughout eastern Europe, for the German agrarian system (because of its inherent advantages) soon spread beyond the strict limits of German colonization, and even in Poland and Lithuania, where the repression of the peasantry was notorious, the German example brought about some amelioration of social conditions. The second consequence more directly affected Germany itself. The creation of a new social structure with manifold advantages over that prevalent in western Germany made for rapid economic development, and consequently the principalities of eastern Germany forged ahead and soon outstripped the politically disjoined west. East of the Elbe the feudal classes, unable to build their power on manorial economy, were politically weak, and the princes did not have to face the opposition of established feudal interests; ruling a population who were free subjects, not feudal dependents, they were able to construct a more modern form of territorial government, unhampered by the survival of early mediaeval theories and practices. Already in the twelfth century Albrecht the Bear (1134-1170), the founder of modern Brandenburg, was 'the freest and most untrammelled prince in Europe'; every inhabitant of his lands, from peasant to baron and bishop, was his subject, and his political authority was simple and complete.[1] But it was at a later stage, in the struggle for power after the death of Frederick II in 1250, that the east colonial lands immediately came to the fore as the seat of political power, usurping the place which had hitherto been claimed by the Rhinelands. The conflict between the Rhenish electors and Albrecht of Austria in 1301 and 1302, in

[1] Cf. Thompson, *op. cit.*, 518-19.

one respect a conflict between elective and hereditary monarchy,[1] was in another respect a struggle for power between old west Germany and the new colonial Germany of the east. From the time of the Interregnum the new dynasties of eastern Germany, the Habsburgs in Austria, the Luxemburgs in Bohemia, the family of Wettin in Meissen, and later the Hohenzollerns in Brandenburg, secured an increasing predominance in German politics. Furthermore, it was in the territories of the north-east and south-east, inhabited by a mixed German and Slav population, that the more concentrated powers came into existence which offset the late-mediaeval decay of government in central and southern Germany. This was still another important factor, for the consolidation of the principalities, which set in after 1356, not only rescued Germany from chaotic conditions but also established the framework in which the history of Germany in modern times was played out.

§ 10. *The Consolidation of the Principalities*

In the fourteenth century Germany appeared rapidly to be sinking into anarchy. Not only was royal authority approaching the verge of extinction, but it seemed as though princely authority, assailed in its turn by the disruptive forces of feudalism, would go the same way as the authority of the emperor. It was not as though the princes, after 1250, succeeded directly to the inheritance of the Hohenstaufen. On the contrary, their strivings for autonomy had weakened the whole structure of government, fractured its monarchical framework, severed the old political bonds and left a void which only new political and administrative developments could fill. But the princes themselves for long made little effort at reconstruction. The political struggle between 1272 and 1356 absorbed their efforts, and so long as they were fishing in troubled waters, struggling for political power against each other and against the emperor, they could not take a firm stand against their subordinates, on whom they were dependent for financial and military support. Furthermore the princes, as a body, proved incapable of rising above the feudal outlook of their dependents, and treated their territories as private properties, to be divided and sub-divided at will. As a result many

---

[1] Cf. above, p. 29.

principalities were soon reduced to insignificant proportions, incapable of healthy political life.[1]

The territorial divisions, reducing the power of the princely dynasties and involving them in internecine struggles, played directly into the hands of the feudal classes, and the result was a second wave of feudalism in Germany, in which the knight class consolidated its power, and banded together in leagues and assemblies to resist princely authority and in particular to resist taxation. At the same time the towns, exploiting their control of ready money, asserted their independence. In north Germany the Hanseatic League pursued its own interests without reference to the territorial princes to whom the member-cities were theoretically subject. In the south there were unions of urban communities — most famous of all the Swabian-Rhenish League of 1381 — to resist encroachments by the princes, and soon knights and cities united for the mutual protection of their rights and privileges. In Brandenburg this occurred as early as 1345, in Lower Bavaria and the county of Mark in 1347, in the Tyrol in 1362; while in Bavaria and Austria there were meetings of all three estates — towns, knights and clergy — in 1394 and 1406.

By the end of the fourteenth century, therefore, the Estates had acquired a definite place in German institutions. Through periodic meetings and the appointment of permanent committees to watch over their interests, they had become a power in the land with which the princes had to negotiate and bargain. Thus there began what is known as the period of 'dualism' in German history, with estates and princes facing each other, often in open hostility, as two independent powers in the land. There has been some tendency in the past to idealize this period, and particularly to emphasize the undeniable cultural and economic achievements of the German cities; and it is true that there was intense life and activity in fourteenth-century Germany. But it was like the undisciplined growth in a garden when the hand of the gardener has been removed; there were many fine

---

[1] No example is more typical than Bavaria which, following the division into Upper and Lower Bavaria in 1255, suffered for over two centuries from the disunity and conflicts within its ruling dynasty. In particular the death of the emperor Ludwig of Bavaria in 1347 ushered in a period of internal strife and division, which left ineradicable marks. Already in 1349 the duchy, which had been reunited in 1340, was divided into three parts; in 1353 Lower Bavaria was redivided. In 1392 the same fate overtook Upper Bavaria, and the net result was to reduce what had once been a great duchy into four petty principalities: Munich and Ingolstadt, Landshut and Straubing. Cf. H. Spangenberg, *Vom Lehnstaat zum Ständestaat* (1912), 49, 101 sqq.

blooms, but their development was marred by lack of space and on the whole the rank growths tended to crowd out the finer plants. The independence of the towns enriched German life, as in a sense all free associations enrich life; but their policy meant a further multiplication of petty autonomies in a land already in fragments, it increased the number of small communities pursuing selfish ends, added to internal divisions, and impaired any chance of common political action. Thus the picture at the end of the fourteenth century, in spite of the appearance of much that was new and valuable in itself, was one of growing confusion, increasing disorder and rampant particularism. This decay was emphasized by the emergence of social cleavages and economic retrogression, bringing conflict between town- and country-dwellers and a struggle within the towns between the urban patriciate and the craft-guilds. Impoverished knights, ruined by the rising cost of living, openly took to banditry, and unrest, lawlessness, violence and insecurity became the keynotes of existence. It was a state of affairs common to the whole of western Europe at the time; but owing to the unhealthy development of the German political system, the lack of an effective central government and the unbridled conflicts of equal powers, it was in Germany that the social turmoil and disorder which everywhere marked the passing of the middle ages, reached their peak.

From this low level Germany was rescued by the princes; and herein we may rightly see their main positive contribution to German history. In later centuries the princely régime became a hard crust stifling the life of Germany beneath; but at the end of the fourteenth century the first necessity was the establishment of an effective civil authority which would really rule, would protect the weak, resolve the conflicts between towns and countryside, control class struggles, and restore peace and security for persons, property and the communications on which social life depended. So much, in a slow and painful process, performed piecemeal and with many setbacks, the princes achieved. From the beginning of the fifteenth century they set about the task of asserting their authority over their subjects, destroying the privileges of the feudal classes and the towns, rounding off and consolidating their territorial possessions, creating for themselves the prerogatives and resources of monarchs, and establishing within their lands the same sort of authority as Henry VIII established for the Tudor dynasty in England. The Golden

Bull of 1356, with its rules on primogeniture and the indivisibility of electoral territories, marked the beginning of this political renaissance; for although strictly applicable only to the seven electorates, its stipulations were soon widely applied in other principalities. A second factor was the spread of Roman law with its principles of the inalienability of public rights and offices, the indivisible authority of the state, and the sovereign will of the prince. A third was the use of cannon and gunpowder, which with other changes in the art of war ended the military predominance of the knighthood; when Frederick I of Hohenzollern defeated the unruly nobility of Brandenburg in 1414, his victory spelt the doom of the feudal castle and of aristocratic independence. When his successor, Frederick II, forced the commune of Berlin in 1442 to surrender its privileges and forbade all leagues of cities within the Mark, save with the prince's consent, it was the beginning of a policy of enforcing control over all associations, which was soon adopted elsewhere. The Elector of Trier, petitioning pope and emperor in 1456 to annul an association of the estates of his territory because it was in conflict with his own sovereign rights, the emperor's majesty and the pope's honour, was only expressing the common attitude of contemporary princes.

A mere mention must suffice of the princes who, imbued with new ideas of government, set themselves the task of turning their scattered broken territories into consolidated territorial states. Among the more notable were Albrecht Achilles of Brandenburg (1471-1486), promulgator of the famous Hohenzollern family law of 1473 confining the electoral dignity exclusively to the eldest son; Henry the Rich of Lower Bavaria who restored the finances of his land and thus laid the foundations for the constructive work of his successor, Ludwig (1450-1479); Matthias Corvinus, king of Hungary (1458-1490), who, as ruler of Silesia after 1469, was the creator of a Silesian constitution; Frederick the Victorious of the Palatinate (1449-1476), who strove to re-unite the principality which had been split into four parts in 1410; Albrecht the Wise of Upper Bavaria (1467-1508), a true forerunner of the enlightened absolutism of the eighteenth century; and finally duke Magnus of Mecklenburg (1477-1503) who, in the words of an orator at his funeral, cured the ills of his land with fire and iron. The work of all these princes had much in common. All strove to introduce primogeniture and the indivisibility of their lands; all strove to create orderly finances, based upon general taxes granted by the assembled estates; all strove to replace local assemblies, the strongholds of aristocratic particularism, by States-General or *Landtage*, representative of the whole principality, and to prevent meetings of the estates except when summoned for a specific purpose by the prince. That purpose was usually to assent to taxation; and the regular meetings of the States-General for the purpose of taxation marked a turning-point in the history of the German principalities. Assemblies which had arisen in the fourteenth century simply for the defence of aristocratic and urban privileges took their place in the scheme of government as a regular vehicle for reconciling the needs of government and the interests of the subjects. The 'dualism' which was characteristic of fourteenth-century Germany was not eradicated; its historical roots were too strong for that, the action of free associations too firmly embedded in German political life. But it was 'canalized' or diverted into new and useful channels. Incorporated in the *Landtage*, the estates provided a counterpart to the independent power of the princes, thus establishing in Germany the elements of a balanced constitution. Furthermore, the regular meetings of the States-General inculcated in their members a new sense of common interests and solidarity; they were an instrument for welding together the haphazard agglomerations of domains, fiefs, counties and lordships, from which most of the principalities developed, and for restoring political unity.

By the end of the fifteenth century the internal situation in Germany was very different from that at the beginning. The revival of princely authority not only provided a necessary counter-balance to the power and divergent interests of the estates, but also created the conditions for the establishment of a balanced constitutional form of government. So long as the princes were weak and lacking in all consciousness of their mission, the estates had the upper hand; but as they gradually recovered power and purpose, a new balance was achieved in which princes and estates each played their part. It is only right to recognize that this progress was due in all essentials to the princes. It was the princes who restored calm to the land by assuming responsibility for the maintenance of public peace. It was they who attacked the spirit of local particularism, who called in Roman law and Roman lawyers against the stagnant force of inherited custom. It was because the princes put their own house in order that they were in a position to strike a balance with the free estates and the economically powerful cities. It was the princes who created the *Landtage* or States-General, forcing the old existing associations into a constitutional mould. In the half-century between 1450 and 1500 they raised Germany out of its inherited anarchy, and laid down the fundamental lines which the constitutional structure of Germany followed down to the nineteenth century. It is here that we must seek the fundamental contribution of the period 1356-1519 to Germany's future. After Charles IV (1346-1378) the history of kings and emperors is trivial and ephemeral; there are no outstanding personalities like Frederick I or Frederick II of Hohenstaufen, and few notable events. It is a period without obvious unity, filled with restless but apparently purposeless activity. Yet below the surface a pattern gradually becomes clear; and this pattern, once the mould had set, was stamped on the body of Germany for centuries to come. With the consolidation of the principalities, which was assured by the end of the fifteenth century, developments reaching back to the Interregnum of 1250-1272 and beyond found their completion, and German history was set finally and irrevocably on a new course. The victory of the princes over the empire was registered for all time in the Golden Bull of 1356; their victory over the forces of dissolution springing from below was registered in the emergence, by the reign of Maximilian I (1493-1519), of the sovereign territorial states.

Chapter III

FROM THE REFORMATION TO THE FALL OF THE HOLY ROMAN EMPIRE
(1519-1806)

§ 11. *Germany on the Eve of the Reformation*

COMPARED with the developments traced in the preceding chapter, which had in them the seeds of the future, the history of the empire in the fifteenth century, down to the accession of Maximilian I in 1493, is a pitiful tale of dissension, debility and disintegration. As the power of the princes in their territories was consolidated, that of the king correspondingly declined. During the fifty years following the death of the emperor Sigismund in 1437 the monarchy fell into an insignificance unparalleled since the Interregnum. Already in 1424 the electoral princes had sought to establish themselves as a permanent supervisory body controlling the exercise of the emperor's powers; in 1438, after the death of the last Luxemburg monarch, they utilized the change of dynasty to impose stringent conditions on the newly elected emperor, Albrecht II. In these circumstances it is no wonder that cautious princes, weighing the burdens of office against the meagre material advantages, were prone to decline the offer of the imperial throne.[1] Carrying with it neither domains nor income, the disendowed empire was too onerous a commitment for the minor princes of Germany and fell almost of course to a ruler whose non-German lands enabled him to bear its burden.[2]

Those who took the royal and imperial title did so primarily with a view to furthering their own dynastic interests or the interests of their hereditary lands. This was true of Charles IV, whose candidature in opposition to Ludwig of Bavaria in 1346 was inspired by fear of losing the Tyrol, and who never ceased throughout the thirty years

---

[1] Of landgrave Ludwig of Hesse, who refused candidature after the death of Albrecht II in 1439, it was said: 'maluit parvo imperio a parentibus sibi relicto utiliter praeesse quam magnum accipiens dissipare'.

[2] A modern writer has likened the emperor to 'the incumbent of a living which was too poorly paid to be held by anyone without private means'.

of his reign to pursue the interests of the Luxemburg dynasty and the Bohemian crown. Charles' outstanding acquisition was the province of Brandenburg; but scarcely less important gains were Silesia and the march of Lausitz, and in the south the frontiers of Bohemia were pushed forward almost to the gates of Nürnberg by the annexation of the lands of the Palatinate along the Bohemian

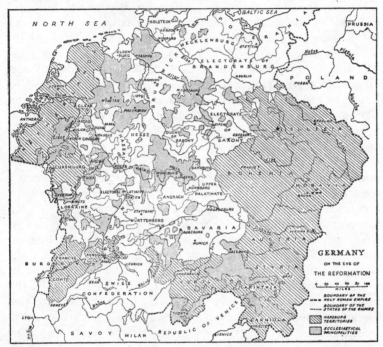

GERMANY
ON THE EVE OF
THE REFORMATION

0   20   40   60   80   100
MILES

BOUNDARY OF THE
HOLY ROMAN EMPIRE
BOUNDARY OF THE
STATES OF THE EMPIRE
HAPSBURG
TERRITORIES
ECCLESIASTICAL
PRINCIPALITIES

borders. All these, for Charles, were additions not to his imperial domain but to the Bohemian kingdom, just as his succession treaty with Austria and the betrothal of his younger son, Sigismund, to the heiress of the king of Hungary and Poland were planned with an eye to Bohemian interests and policy. Far from identifying Bohemia with the Reich, Charles sought to increase the independence of his kingdom, which he hoped to make the nucleus of a predominantly Slav empire reaching from the Elbe to the Lower Danube and east to the Vistula: to emphasize Bohemian independence, the subordination of the church of Prague to the archbishopric of Mainz was abolished in 1344, and a new archbishopric created which was given the prerogative of consecrating and crowning the Bohemian king.

In so far as the only practical basis of the German kingship in this era was the territorial power of the ruling sovereign, Charles IV's Bohemian policy served Germany well, and the words of Adalbert of Prague, in his funeral oration after Charles' death, fairly sum up the achievements of the reign: 'so held he his power in Bohemia and the empire', said the archbishop, 'that neither the empire lacked order nor Bohemia lacked care, and the men of the empire were content and the men of Bohemia found no cause for complaint.' It was otherwise under Charles' sons, Wenzel (1378-1400) and Sigismund (1410-1437). So long as dynastic policy prospered, it helped to stabilize the monarchy; but after Charles' death in 1378 all the difficulties inherent in a complicated, ambitious dynastic policy began to be felt. In 1382 the question of the Hungarian and Polish succession arose, involving the house of Luxemburg in continued warfare. More important, Bohemia itself became the scene of reaction and civil war. In the first place, the aristocracy sought to recover the predominance lost under Charles, and to prevent a further strengthening of the monarchy in league with the towns and the lesser nobility. Secondly, the deliberate emphasis on Bohemian nationalism, which ran consistently through Charles' policy, provoked an anti-German reaction, which took violently nationalist shape when the Hussite movement added religious to political animosity. These complications, threatening to unseat the dynasty in its hereditary lands, absorbed the energies of Wenzel and Sigismund, and Germany was inevitably neglected. Characteristically the emperor, embroiled in the Hussite wars, refused to give active support to the Teutonic Order in its struggle with Poland.[1] The German lands of the dynasty also suffered from the absence of the ruler; in particular the aristocracy got the upper hand in Brandenburg, and the work of the Ascanian dynasty was undone.[2] Among the causes leading to Wenzel's deposition in 1400 none was weightier than the king's continued residence in Bohemia outside

---

[1] Cf. above, p. 42.

[2] On the early history of Brandenburg, cf. above, p. 45. The decline of the march began after the extinction of the Ascanian dynasty in 1319, when Louis of Bavaria sought to obtain the province for the Wittelsbachs. The subsequent contests for possession and the concessions made to secure support inevitably played into the hands of the aristocracy, whose power reached its peak under Sigismund's absentee rule.

the borders of the German kingdom. Already in 1395, when Wenzel in spite of all complaints had already absented himself from Germany for seven years, the question of deposition was ventilated; and the nomination of Sigismund as imperial vicar the following year did nothing to lessen discontent, since he was fully occupied with the Hungarian question. But the unhappy interlude of Rupert's reign (1400-1410) proved for all time the impotence of a king without broad domains of his own, and particularly the weakness of a king from western Germany in face of the princes of the north and east; and on Rupert's death the electors, almost of necessity,[1] turned again to the house of Luxemburg and elected Sigismund (1410-1437). In practice, no other course was feasible; but the result was that, for still another generation, Germany was neglected while the king strove to restore his position within Bohemia.

The change of dynasty after the death of Sigismund in 1437 brought no immediate improvement. Albrecht of Habsburg (1438-1439), the husband of Sigismund's only daughter, Elizabeth, succeeded as the heir of the house of Luxemburg; but he was also heir to all the complications the Bohemian inheritance carried with it. Moreover, Habsburg power was at a low ebb. The rule of primogeniture, which from the time of Rudolf I had secured the Habsburgs pre-eminence among the princes of Germany, had lapsed in 1379 and thenceforward there were two Habsburg lines, the one ruling Austria proper, the latter (which was soon subdivided) in control of the minor Habsburg territories. These divisions and the consequent family strife and discord were accentuated by Albrecht's early death, and persisted through the long reign of his successor, Frederick III (1440-1493). The effects of these discords within Austria were such as we are already familiar with in other princely territories: civil war led by opposing branches of the ruling dynasty, leagues of recalcitrant knights, the rise of provincial estates and the predominance of particularist interests. But the fact that Frederick was not only ruler of Austria but also king of Germany implicated the whole Reich in his problems. Scarcely able to maintain himself in his hereditary lands, Frederick

---

[1] The throne was offered to Henry IV of England — a belated flicker of a policy common in the thirteenth and fourteenth centuries, and another example of the necessity of finding a foreign monarch to bear the burden — but he declined the offer.

E

was still less able to safeguard the interests and frontiers of Germany. Hence his reign, like that of Sigismund before him, was characterized by growing restrictions on royal power and influence within, and by manifest weakness on all the frontiers.

Within Germany the first half of the fifteenth century was notable for the withdrawal of the monarchy from the colonial lands of the north. The Wittelsbachs and the early Luxemburgs, with a quick eye for the seat of political power, had sought an entry into the north, particularly the march of Brandenburg, hoping thereby to consolidate their position and secure a broader and more lasting foundation for the monarchy. Under Sigismund this policy — which still, until the end of the fourteenth century, carried with it some hope of greater political stability and even ultimately of a restoration of royal power — was abandoned. Engrossed in the problems of Bohemia and Hungary, in dire need of money and allies, and in despair of governing the land, which had become more of a liability than an asset, Sigismund made Frederick of Hohenzollern, burgrave of Nürnberg, his lieutenant in the march of Brandenburg and later, in 1415, created him Elector in reward for his services. More immediately important was his decision in 1423 to confer the electorate and duchy of Saxony, vacant through the extinction of the house of Saxe-Wittenberg, on his staunchest ally in the Hussite wars, Frederick of Meissen. It was more than two centuries before Brandenburg, under the Great Elector (1640-1688), began to recover from late-mediaeval anarchy; but the junction of Meissen, with its flourishing mining industries the most prosperous principality of mediaeval Germany, and the electorate of Saxony created a powerful state which, in the early sixteenth century, was to assume the leadership of the Protestant north against the Habsburgs. The immediate result of Sigismund's actions, however, was that the north was left to go its own way, and in fact (though not in theory) the cleavage between north and south, which had been resisted throughout the middle ages, was consummated. Only time and events could determine whether this cleavage was to be permanent; but with the imperial title vested, from the election of Albrecht II in 1438 to the end of the old Reich in 1806, in the Habsburg dynasty, every year that passed tended to drive home its implications and render it more durable.

What men saw and felt in the fifteenth century, however, was not the breach in German unity — which, in fact, it took centuries to consummate — but the weakness which overtook German policy on all its frontiers. Large portions of the borderlands were either drifting away from the Reich or linked by only the loosest of bonds. By the Peace of Thorn (1466) the Teutonic Order, weakened and despoiled, became a vassal of Poland. In the north-west Holstein was associated by personal union with Denmark, and moved in a Danish orbit. On the eastern frontier, the agreement of 1436 by which Sigismund finally secured recognition in Bohemia, left that country virtually independent under nominal German overlordship; and even this precarious settlement failed to last. In 1458, native rulers were elected both in Bohemia and in Hungary, and Frederick III was not long in granting them formal recognition. Thus the union of Austria, Bohemia and Hungary, which had cost the Habsburgs so much effort, was destroyed. Disintegration went a step further when, in 1468, Matthias Corvinus of Hungary set out to conquer Bohemia, while Poland also fished in troubled waters. The upshot on the death of the Bohemian king, George Podiebrad, in 1471 was a partition for the benefit of Poland and Hungary; the Polish prince received Bohemia itself, while the neighbouring provinces of Moravia, Silesia and Lausitz were incorporated in Hungary. Frederick III meanwhile stood aside helpless, his own Austrian lands threatened by Matthias, who conquered and occupied Vienna in 1485. Nor, if such was the situation in the east, was the position in the west any healthier. As early as 1415 the Swiss of the 'Eight Ancient Cantons', who (profiting from internal dissensions within the house of Habsburg) had already conquered most of the Habsburg lands south of the Rhine, obtained full internal autonomy from Sigismund; as the fifteenth century proceeded successful wars with the dukes of Burgundy and Savoy increased their power, and from 1495 they assumed an attitude of independence which, stalwartly maintained, was formally recognized in 1648. At the same time the power of Burgundy was steadily rising to its culmination under Charles the Bold (1467-1477). After the union of Brabant with Flanders and Burgundy in 1430, the Burgundian dynasty reached out more and more after imperial lands: Hainault was annexed in 1433, Luxemburg in 1451, then the diocese of Liége and Guelders. In 1469 duke Sigismund of Habsburg handed over Upper Alsace for a money payment; in 1473 the duke of Lorraine was forced to allow the Burgundians to occupy all strongholds throughout his land. Finally in 1474 Charles the Bold sought to annex the electorate of Cologne. Meanwhile France, although threatened as much as the empire by the rise of Burgundian power, was striking out on its own; the end of the Hundred Years War with England left it free to resume the Capetian policy of eastward expansion, and in 1444 a French army appeared in Lorraine and Alsace, took up winter quarters, demanded the submission of Metz and Strassburg, and launched an attack on Basel.

Such, in summary retrospect, was the position on Germany's frontiers on the eve of the reign of Maximilian I (1493-1519). On the one side, Cologne and Strassburg were in danger; on the other Vienna. The princes, intent on their own tasks, were indifferent. Frederick II of Brandenburg alone had any perception of the situation. Seeking to establish his dynasty along the shores of the Baltic by marriages and pacts with Lauenburg, Pomerania and Mecklenburg, he offered to expel the Danes from German soil if the emperor would grant him Holstein; but Vienna's answer was a curt rebuff. As for the emperor Frederick III, he had neither the will nor the means to cope with the situation. In the east he watched uneasily the rise of Matthias Corvinus of Hungary, consoling himself with the fact that Matthias was childless and that by an Austro-Hungarian treaty of 1463, if either house were to die out, the other was to succeed to its inheritance. In the west, similar calculations governed his relations with Burgundy: Charles the Bold had only one daughter, and Frederick's plan was to secure the Burgundian inheritance by a marriage between her and his own son, Maximilian. There is no sign in these dynastic schemes of any attempt either to calculate realistically the prospects of putting them into effect if the opportunity materialized, or to weigh the cost of straining to incorporate so many heterogeneous territories. In the east, the whole scheme came to nothing by a Hungarian refusal, on the death of Matthias in 1490, to honour the agreement of 1463 — a refusal which neither Frederick nor Maximilian had the means to challenge. In the west it was otherwise. After Charles the Bold's defeat and death at the hands of the Swiss in 1477, the Netherlands diet, in order to protect the country from France, which was determined to lay hands on Charles' inheritance, gave the heiress of Burgundy in marriage to Maximilian.

The Burgundian marriage of 1477 was a turning-point in Habsburg history. It brought back Austria, which was tending more and more to be absorbed in the parochial affairs of south-east Europe, into the main stream of European politics, raised it to a first place among the powers, and gave it a direct interest in western Europe which lasted down to Napoleonic times. For Germany also its consequences were momentous. In the first place, it tied the empire, in Habsburg hands since 1438, irrevocably to Austria. The house of Habsburg was now incomparably stronger than any other German princely family; but it needed the imperial dignity, for only as the reigning imperial house could it knit together and maintain hold over its far-flung territorial possessions stretching from the Lower Rhine and the Scheldt to the Upper Rhine, to the eastern Alps and along the Danube. It could not afford to see another dynasty in possession of the imperial title; for, however weak in itself, such a dynasty would, in alliance with France, constitute a threat to Austrian interests. This was the second direct consequence of the marriage of 1477. France could not be expected to give up the hope of recovering those French lands alienated by the Burgundian dynasty; and with Burgundy, therefore, Austria inherited the perennial hostility of France. This represented almost a revolution in European politics, for in earlier times the house of Austria had usually been found aligned with France for the exploitation of western Germany. Now, in defence of its own interests, it was forced to accept the guardianship of the west against French encroachments; but this threw those states in Germany which were opposed to Habsburg predominance into the arms of France. Hence, through the Franco-Austrian opposition over Burgundy, the empire was involved in foreign complications on a scale hitherto unknown. And yet it was not involved on its own account. For the Habsburgs, Germany was a secondary possession, important only as a connecting link between the dispersed Habsburg territories and as a field on which to assemble forces for war against France. There was no longer any imperial policy except in the sense of Habsburg policy; and Habsburg policy was at best only partially in line with German interests. Thus, in the struggles for predominance which filled the European scene after 1494, Germany sank more and more into the condition of a subordinate factor, a field for annexations and compensations fought over by other states.

That such was the case was amply borne out by the history of the years 1493-1519. Maximilian had been elected King of the Romans in 1486, during his father's lifetime, in the hope that, with the Burgundian inheritance behind him, he would be able to restore peace and union to the empire. The inglorious history of the previous half-century had produced, in reaction, a profound movement of German nationalism without parallel since the Diet of Rhens in 1338. It was now that the saga of the emperor Frederick Barbarossa, slumbering on the Kyffhäuser waiting to restore the empire to its old glory, took hold over popular imagination; a number of pseudo-Fredericks appeared and secured a following. A new, more coherent expression of national consciousness found vent in the work of Humanists like Sebastian Brant and Jacob Wimpfeling, who in his *Epitome Rerum Germanicarum* appealed to Germany's past. The Humanists, well aware of the egoism of the princes, looked to Maximilian to restore inner order and external unity. Superficially, he seemed to have the means and — compared with Frederick — the will. He had started well, reuniting all the Habsburg lands in 1490, and recovering the lost districts of Austria from Hungary; hence he had in his hereditary lands the necessary material basis for the exercise of royal power. Among contemporaries there appears to have been no realization that the very extent and diversity of these territories, without any internal bonds of union, were as much a source of weakness as of strength, and in any event a source of constant preoccupation. From the beginning of his reign Maximilian spent his time defending Habsburg dynastic interests and possessions, particularly his Burgundian kingdom, from France. Burgundy was the corner-stone of his policy. Because of Burgundy, he accepted existing conditions in the east, knowing full well that France would exploit any entanglement with Poland or Hungary or Bohemia to seize his Burgundian lands. Because of Burgundy, he went to war with the French in Italy, fearful of any extension of French power. The succession in 1516 to the Spanish throne of his grandson, Charles — ruler of the Netherlands since 1506 — opened up still greater prospects of Habsburg dynastic aggrandizement; but it also added new complications. It made the imperial title still more necessary as a unifying bond between the Habsburg dominions; but it neither served nor was compatible with German interests. Maximilian did not hesitate, when it served his purpose, to claim that his policy was directed to assuring Germany its proper place among nations and protecting its ancient rights against foreigners; but it is difficult for the scrupulous historian to find in it anything but the dynastic interests of the Habsburg house. More than once he frankly stated that it did not suit his purpose for his hereditary lands to be reckoned in the German Reich.[1] His attempts to drag Germany into his wars with France met stubborn opposition alike from princes and towns, for neither of which was the possession of Milan or Picardy a vital interest.[2]

Thus Maximilian's reign brought to the surface the conflict between Habsburg dynastic policy and German interests, which henceforward was endemic in German history. The hopes of a national policy, in defence of the threatened frontiers, with which the reign opened, proved illusory. Through Burgundy, Austria was already caught up in the whirlpool of European policy; this was even more apparent after Maximilian was succeeded by Charles V in 1519. Inevitably this situation was reflected in German internal affairs. For Maximilian, Germany was primarily a source of supply, to which he looked for the financing of his wars; but it never appears to have entered his calculations that the surest way of securing German financial and political support was to identify his interests with those of the Reich by co-operating in a long-needed measure of internal reform. It was Machiavelli who said that the disproportion between Germany's natural powers and its political capacities was the result of its defective constitution; and for many years before Maximilian's accession the need for constitutional reform was widely ventilated. From 1485 it was the leading issue in the Reichstag; thereafter the question never ceased to occupy men's minds throughout the quarter-century preceding the Reformation. The soul of the movement for reform was Berthold of Henneberg, elector of Mainz, whose plans had at least the merit of taking full account of the existing conditions; by and large his proposals amounted to a scheme for the constitution of a federal state, in which the administration was to be taken out of the hands of the monarchy and placed in those of an imperial council of seventeen members, of which the president alone would be the emperor's nominee. Such a scheme of government was in line with the course of historical development since the

[1] Andreas, *Deutschland vor der Reformation*, 241.
[2] Cf. Haller, *France and Germany* (1932), 23.

Golden Bull; indeed, if there is any truth in the dictum that the
Golden Bull 'legalized anarchy',[1] it may be said that Berthold's plan
was to overcome the anarchy by completing the structure legalized
in 1356 through the addition of the necessary organs of co-ordination
and executive power which the emperor no longer effectively.
possessed outside his hereditary lands. To the reconstituted government it was proposed to give adequate means of action by reforming
the judicature, the imperial finances and the army.

The project of 'Reichsreform', which was fully debated in the
Reichstag of 1495, where it won the support of practically every
prince and estate, has been much criticized. It was, it has been said,[2]
an attempt to carry further the 'diminution of the central power
through permanent institutions'; in the eyes of the princes it was
simply 'the means of assuring and enlarging their own share in the
government of the realm'. But we do not need to overrate the
altruism of the princes to see that there was more to it than this. The
movement which bore the project forward drew its force from
circles far wider than the prince's courts; it reflected the genuine
aspirations of the German people. Moreover, permanent institutions
far from diminishing the effete central power which had already sunk
to its lowest point during the long reign of Frederick III, provided
the only hope of more effective government beyond the narrow
limits of the princely territories. The creation, in 1500 and 1512, of
ten provincial districts (*Kreise*) comprising each a number of separate
principalities, was, despite its limited objects, a step towards greater
territorial cohesion, just as the proposal at the Reichstag of 1522-1523
to raise a general imperial customs duty (*Reichsgrenzzoll*) implied
recognition of the empire as a single economic unit. All this went
beyond the immediate dynastic interests of the princes, as fundamentally did the plans for the reconstruction of imperial taxation.
A conflict of interests there was over the methods and form of
taxation, one party favouring a poll-tax (*gemeiner Pfennig*), the other
the levying of contributions by the individual cities and principalities,
each of which was left free to decide how it would collect and pay
its contribution; but the very fact that they were willing to put
imperial finances on a stable foundation showed that the princes still
accepted, and were prepared to make tangible concessions on behalf

---

[1] Bryce, *Holy Roman Empire* (ed. 1928), 246.
[2] Cf. Haller, *Epochs of German History*, 110-111.

of, a form of federal state which transcended the boundaries and immediate interests of their principalities.

In view of these considerations it is difficult to stand aside and view the struggle over 'Reichsreform' as simply the expression of the conflicting interests of princes, autonomous cities and emperor, in which all parties were equally intent on self-aggrandizement. On the contrary, the attempt at reform was serious; and although, in view of the complicated state of political organization in Germany, many difficulties were clearly to be anticipated in putting it into effect, the responsibility for the failure to give it a trial rests with Maximilian and his successor, Charles V. Their obtuseness and intransigence threw away the last chance of restoring to Germany a real measure of unity. When Charles V, opening his first Diet at Worms in January 1521, stated that 'the empire from of old has had not many masters, but one, and it is our intention to be that one', and when he added that he was not to be treated as of less account than his predecessors, but of more, seeing that he was more powerful than they had been, he was accusing himself of crass historical romanticism or outlining a policy of compulsion, or both. In either case, he was deliberately setting himself against the whole trend of historical development since the days of Charles IV,[1] and — at the very moment when he needed German support against France — announcing a trial of strength with the princes. It is still often argued that such a trial of strength was, in 1519, far from a hopeless proposition; that the Habsburgs still had the possibility, in view of their wide territories, of enforcing throughout Germany an absolutist régime.[2] Such an argument ignores the external complications, particularly the inevitability of French interference, just as it underrates the progress of the principalities towards consolidation during the latter half of the fifteenth century; still more it forgets that, although the emperor might defeat the German princes by force of Habsburg arms, it was another question to maintain and consolidate his predominance. In 1547 Charles V won complete victory over the German opposition; his position, resting on the arms of his Spanish soldiery, could not have been stronger. But his success lasted only

---

[1] That the Habsburgs were perfectly conscious of this is indicated by Maximilian's verdict on Charles IV: 'Carolo quarto pestilentior pestis nunquam alias contigit Germaniae.'

[2] Andreas, op. cit., 264: 'Als dieser (Maximilian) die Augen schloss, war es noch nicht ausgemacht, ob den Reichsständen fürderhin oder dem Kaisertum die volle Ueberlegenheit zufallen werde.'

until 1552, and was followed by a collapse so rapid that in 1555 Charles had to acknowledge defeat in the Peace of Augsburg.

The events of 1547-1555 are the best proof that the way to German unity did not lie through armed force, and that any revival of the empire must take account of irrevocable historical developments. That Maximilian and Charles ignored this fact was due not only to intransigence and obtuseness, but also to the conflict of Habsburg and German interests. They could not afford to accede to any project of reform because they did not intend to rule and act as German emperors, and a government directed and controlled by a council (*Reichsregiment*) representing the German estates might well be expected, particularly in foreign affairs, to oppose the employment of German resources for the execution of Habsburg dynastic interests and to insist on a German policy. Here, rather than in the constitutional field, was where the fundamental antagonism lay. Hence the Habsburgs were, from the beginning, determined opponents of the reform movement, who skilfully exploited and accentuated the divergent interests of the different estates so as to bring all projects to nothing; and any concessions won from them were the result either of financial embarrassment or of foreign complications. Even projects, like the plan for an imperial customs system, which might have been thought to their advantage, were dismissed, while such concessions as were made under the pressure of external events were temporary manœuvres to which neither Maximilian nor Charles had any intention of according permanent validity. Thus the 'Reichsregiment' set up in 1500 for a period of six years, with competence over all internal and external affairs of the empire, was abolished by Maximilian in 1502, and that established by Charles V in 1521, with powers only during the emperor's absence, scarcely lasted until 1530. The proposal of 1495 for annual meetings of a full *Reichstag*, comprising all estates, was never put into effect. After 1530, under the pressure of the Reformation and the overt hostility between the emperor and the Protestant princes, there was neither interest in, nor were conditions favourable to, peaceful reform: the last opportunity to maintain the unity of Germany by constitutional changes appropriate to the existing political structure had passed, unused and beyond recall.

§ 12. *The Reformation and the Wars of Religion*

The result of the manœuvres of Maximilian and Charles V was that the constitutional problem, as Germany made the transition from mediaeval to modern times, was left unsolved. But the political movement which found expression in the projects of reform was not assuaged. The very negotiations between the emperor and the estates, protracted, complicated and sometimes excited, produced a state of heightened tension and expectancy. The princes, far from resigning themselves to their lack of success under Maximilian, were only the more determined to secure reform from Charles; hence their decision in 1519 to make the election dependent on the acceptance of a 'capitulation' — the first of a series of 'electoral capitulations' which lasted as long as the old empire — which was neither more nor less than a solemn treaty between the emperor-elect and the electoral princes, covering the whole ambit of imperial government and including an undertaking to set up a 'Reichsregiment' composed of representatives of the estates. But the issue of constitutional reform was only a focus for the sense of frustration and discontent with existing conditions which ran much deeper through the whole of German society. The whole nation, wearied of the disunity, incompetence and lack of governance which were the mark of the preceding century, was in a state of political crisis, which was fanned by the work of propagandists and satirists who, in widely-read verse, attacked Rome and the great prelates, the higher social classes and the corruption of the bourgeoisie by money. Nowhere is the common feeling more graphically portrayed than in the works of Dürer, who gave permanent expression to the sense of insecurity, distress and even desperation which ran throughout Germany. Ulrich von Hutten, whose *Epistolae obscurorum virorum*, published in 1514, raised hostility to Rome to a new peak of violence, also bitterly reproached all classes within Germany with betrayal of their country for their own selfish interests. But it was hostility to Rome which aroused and united national consciousness. It was an extraordinary thing, in this age of territorial division, how wide and popular was the support for the *Gravamina nationis Germanicae*, which formulated the complaints of the German nation against Rome. The Humanists had given new life to the words *Germani* and *Germania*, and to the idea of common nationality which they embodied; Maximilian took it up on the political plane and added the words 'of the German Nation' (*Nationis Teutonicae*) to the old title 'Sacred Roman Empire' (*sacrum imperium Romanum*), thus seeking to give his imperial dignity a national flavour. But, after the disappointment on the political plane, the frustrated hopes of constitutional reform, it was in the religious reformation that the new spirit of German nationalism found expression.

The age produced, in Luther, a figure who transcended his generation; but Luther was fortunate in finding the times propitious. That the reformation occurred when and where it did was no accident of history; Luther's challenge in the famous Wittenberg 'theses' of 1517 was transformed in a trice from an academic controversy into a burning popular issue because it found an echo in the revolutionary movement fomenting in Germany. The *Gravamina* of 1518 showed that Luther had at his back the whole German people, in spite of the territorial fragmentation of Germany. His challenge to Rome appealed to the national consciousness, disappointed and frustrated by the years of haggling and bargaining over 'Reichsreform'. His belief that the essence of religion lay in an inner experience was in the German tradition of Meister Eckardt, Dietrich of Strassburg and Thomas à Kempis — a mystical tradition in no way purely German, but especially rife in Germany from the fourteenth century onwards because nowhere else were political and social conditions such that the only freedom left to the common man was the inner freedom of the spirit. Believing that the essence of religion lay in spiritual experience, Luther sought to unite the German emperor, princes, clergy and people against the stifling juridical system administered from Rome; he opposed the spiritual Church to the 'human' institutions of the papacy, councils, episcopate and canon law. His appeal was to the 'German nation', to the 'Christian nobility of the German nation'. He planned, of course, to reform the universal Church; but the resistance of Rome threw him back increasingly on German support and gave his propaganda a peculiarly German flavour. 'It is for you Germans', he wrote in 1531, 'that I seek salvation and sanctity.'

The response swept the whole country. A generation later, writing in 1557-1559, the Venetian ambassadors reported that nine-tenths of Germany was Protestant and that it was only a question of time before the whole country would belong to the new faith. But the effects of the movement, corresponding to the forces behind it, extended far beyond the sphere of religion. Luther's appeal, reaching across the outward barriers of territorial particularism, put fresh life into the disjointed body of Germany. His translation of the Bible gave common currency to the new form of the German language, which — springing up in the colonial east, where settlers from all parts of Germany were mingled — had slowly found its way into the chanceries of Vienna and Saxony and Brandenburg, at the same period as a common tongue was gaining ascendancy in England over the provincial dialects. Through Luther's Bible, with its vigorous, positive vocabulary, the bond of common language, replacing provincial dialects, became a factor of unity in Germany; the same result was achieved by his treatises addressed to the people in their thousands which (like the subsequent controversial writings of his partisans and adversaries) propagated far and wide a speech common to all Germans. In his manifesto of 1520 'To the Christian nobility of the German nation on the improvement of the Christian condition' he drew up a programme of religious reform applicable to the whole of Germany and called upon the princes of the empire — 'the Christian nobility' — to put it into effect. But his teachings, with their appeal to first principles and their incitement to question the established order, were immediately applied to social and economic, as well as to religious affairs. The hope of immediate, radical change, cutting short the interminable controversy between the emperor and the estates, which Lutheranism aroused, found its earliest expression in a rising among the smaller knights — a class whose economic depression we have already noted[1] — which took place in 1522-1523. A few months later, in 1524, the Peasants' War broke out in south-west Germany, only to be crushed under the superior military power of the nobility.

Thus the early decades of the sixteenth century witnessed in Germany a revolutionary ferment which, in reaction against the decline of the empire in the last two or three generations, was strongly national in character. In appealing to the German nation, Luther was at least in part in revolt against the particularism of the princes, the pretensions of the nobility and the egoism of the townsfolk and peasantry. Humanists like Hutten, because they were

[1] Above, p. 48.

nationalists, were initially faithful — often to the point of illusory romanticism — to the empire. But the emperor, who had failed to grasp the fleeting chance of constitutional reform, turned his back on the opportunity of placing himself at the head of the national movement. That such an opportunity was there to be taken is beyond doubt; but once again, deeper than any individual repugnance to the new doctrines or personal loyalty to Rome, the conflict of German and Habsburg interests was the stumbling-block. Charles V, the king of Spain, whose real power derived from his non-German lands,[1] could not afford to compromise his position outside Germany by placing himself at the head of a German movement directed against Rome. He was a Habsburg first, King of Spain next, and only at long last the German emperor. Hence, although committed to the principles of Church reform and steeped in the conciliar traditions of the fifteenth century, Charles determined from the first to suppress the reform movement, such hesitation and delay as there was being due solely to foreign complications.

The movement which had within it, even at that late date, the seeds of German unity, thus became the cause of dissension, war and division. The political history of the German reformation is so familiar that only the salient points need mention: the Edict of Worms in 1521, placing Luther under the imperial ban; the approval, under imperial pressure, of the edict of 1521 by a majority at the Diet of Speyer in 1529 and the resultant protest by a number of the most influential members; the failure of the Diet of Augsburg in 1530 to restore unity and the formation of the Protestant League; the outbreak of civil war in 1546 (after a long delay due to the appearance of the Turkish armies before Vienna and war with France) and Charles' ephemeral victory in 1547; the revolt of the Protestants under Maurice of Saxony in 1552, followed in 1555 by the Peace of Augsburg. As early as 1521 and 1522 the practical measures of reform which Luther had demanded in his appeal to the Christian nobility — the sequestration of Church property, the overthrow of Church authorities, the abolition of celibacy, etc. — had everywhere begun, and in 1526 the Diet of Speyer charged every estate in the empire to conduct itself in the ecclesiastical issue according to the dictates of its

---

[1] His minister, Granvella, informed the Diet of Speyer that 'the emperor has, for the support of his dignity, not a hazel-nut's worth of profit from the empire'.

own conscience, thus deliberately turning over the decision of the religious question to each province and territory separately. This decision, resisted for so long by Charles, was accepted as the basis of the compromise of 1555: except for the heads of ecclesiastical states, who were not permitted to change to the reformed faith, each prince was given the right to decide the religion of his principality, and with the organization of the two parties into two bodies in the imperial Diet an uneasy equilibrium was reached, which lasted — due in part to the decline of Habsburg fortunes and their constant difficulties in the east — into the seventeenth century. Nevertheless the progress of Protestantism continued, especially in north Germany, where no Catholic dynasty remained, and where one bishopric after another was absorbed until by 1577 only Hildesheim was left. Simultaneously the Catholic counter-reformation began. In 1573 the prince-abbot of Dernbach forced the Protestant knights of his domains to return to the Catholic faith; in 1574 the archbishop of Mainz followed his example. A decade later the same issue arose at Cologne; and the intervention of Spanish troops secured the Westphalian bishoprics for Catholicism. When, in 1608, duke Maximilian of Bavaria, the acknowledged Catholic leader, annexed the town of Donauwörth and forced it to accept the Catholic faith, the whole issue once more became perilous. Under the leadership of the Palatinate, the Evangelical Union was formed for the defence of the religious peace; Bavaria replied in 1609 with the creation of the Catholic League. All that was wanting was Habsburg intervention. The emperor Matthias (1612-1619) clung to a policy of mediation, but already by 1617 he had been ousted for all practical purposes by his cousin, Ferdinand of Styria, and when in 1619 Ferdinand was elected emperor the immediate outbreak of civil war could be foreseen.

Once again only a recapitulation of a bare outline of events between 1618 and 1648 is necessary. The struggle opened with revolt in Bohemia, where the counter-reformation simultaneously violated religious feeling and ancient privileges, and the uprising soon spread to Austria. It became a German issue when, in 1619, the Elector Palatine, the leader of the Protestant faction, decided to accept the Bohemian crown at the hands of the rebels. After his annihilating defeat at the battle of the White Mountain, near Prague, in 1620, the war was carried into Germany; Bavaria, which had given

Ferdinand the active support of the Catholic League, wanted 'compensation' in the form of the lands of the Upper Palatinate and the electoral dignity; the Spaniards wanted Alsace and the Rhenish Palatinate. From the Palatinate, where Catholic arms were successful, the war was carried into north Germany, and the peace of Lübeck (1629) constituted the high water mark of Ferdinand's power. But the appearance of Spanish Catholicism on the shores of the Baltic constituted a threat to Protestant Sweden, whose whole position rested on the control of the Baltic seas, just as the Spaniards in the Rhineland were a direct threat to France. The invasion of Germany by Gustavus Adolphus of Sweden in 1630 marked the turn of the tide; his alliance with France in 1631 was another milestone in the decline of Habsburg fortunes; and when finally, after Gustavus' death in 1632, France took up arms in 1635, the issue was sealed. Militarily, the Habsburgs were defeated by 1646; but the war dragged on another two years, until it was brought to a close by the Peace of Westphalia.

The treaties of 1648 closed the epoch which began in 1519. Every hope and project inspiring the wave of revolutionary ardour which swept Germany at the beginning of the sixteenth century, had been disappointed. A movement which began as a reaction against foreign intervention, and the internal weakness which permitted foreign intervention, resulted in its last phases in foreign intervention on a scale hitherto unknown. Instead of a restoration, on new and more solid foundations, of a common political and administrative organization for the whole of Germany — an organization which, while taking account of the consolidation of the principalities, would have permitted common action on a federal basis in common problems — the peace of 1648 consecrated the sovereignty of the principalities; after 1648 the subordination of the principalities within the empire was a form of words without political significance, the empire a shadow without substance, beyond all hope of resurrection or reform. A religious movement which, for a short generation, seemed to offer a new bond of unity to the German peoples, where political bonds had failed, was transformed instead, through the opposition of the Habsburgs, into a new cause of division; particularly during the Thirty Years War the breach between Lutherans and Calvinists opened nearly as wide as the chasm between Catholics and Protestants. Confessional dualism allied itself with territorial fragmentation, and the spiritual exaltation which had found expression in the Reformation faded into apathy or turned away into channels remote from politics. Finally Germany suffered the ravages of civil war and the miseries of a Franco-Spanish war fought with unbelievable brutality on German soil.[1] The Thirty Years War decimated the population,[2] depressed the peasants and ruined the towns, and thus changed the whole social and economic substructure of German political life. In this, it only carried a stage further the consequences of the religious wars of the sixteenth century, which had been in large measure consolidated during the uneasy peace between 1555 and 1618; but, taking the period 1519–1648 as a whole, the result was a transformation of German society. The weakening of all classes in town and country, which was the inevitable consequence of generations of strife, the effect of war on commerce, industry and agriculture, brought about, with the religious changes, a further rise in the power of the princes, which ushered in the period of princely absolutism.

§ 13. *The Rise of Absolutism*

We saw, at the end of the last chapter, how by the close of the fifteenth century a new stability and balance had been struck within the territorial states of Germany; we saw, in particular, the beginnings of a fruitful co-operation between princes and estates, which boded well for a healthy development of political life and institutions on a basis of progressive 'constitutionalism'.[3] This promise of healthy constitutional development within the territorial states, offsetting in some degree the ills of the imperial constitution, withered away in the storms which accompanied and followed the Reformation.

In the first place, the Reformation itself upset the balance by creating new sources of princely authority. Historians are in the main agreed that Luther himself had no intention of subordinating

---

[1] They are powerfully described in Grimmelshausen's famous novel, *Simplicissimus* (Engl. translation, 1912).

[2] It has been estimated that the number of Germans fell by half or two-thirds, or from more than 16,000,000 to less than 6,000,000. The credibility of the latter figure was accepted by von Inama-Sternegg ('Die volkswirthschaftlichen Folgen des Dreissigjährigen Kriegs', *Hist. Taschenbuch*, 1864), whose work is the basis of the statements of most subsequent writers; but the unreliability of the data for all such estimates should not be forgotten.

[3] Above, p. 50.

F

the Church to the secular power; he was no Erastian, and wanted an independent Church. But the circumstances under, and the methods by which the Reformation was carried out, forced his hands. The unswerving opposition of Charles V compelled him to seek the help of the princes — Frederick the Wise of Saxony to the fore — and, as we have observed, the practical measures of reform in 1521-1522 were carried out by the princes on their own initiative. Frightened by the social unrest of the Peasants' Wars, which was an unwanted consequence of his preaching, Luther sided wholeheartedly with the princes in their suppression, and thus placed himself even more closely under their influence. Moreover, his doctrinal position was not altogether unequivocal: preaching an invisible and purely spiritual Church, in radical opposition to the juridical institutions of Rome, he was led to concede that the state is the form in which, under God's will, the world exists, and that, since ecclesiastical institutions were but the work of man, with no authority in divine law, the state had full right to shape them and make them its own. Thus in the end, partly under duress, partly through the ambiguity of his position, he left to the prince authority over persons, consistories, parishes, pastors, over ecclesiastical properties and even over the forms of religious service and dogma. In brief, the prince became the *summus episcopus* of his territorial Church, and enlisted its resources in support of his territorial power. It was the princes who decided such matters as the Confession of Augsburg or the Articles of Smalkald. They took advantage of the political conflicts aroused by the Reformation to bind the new churches to the secular power and make of them the most solid supports of their sovereignty.

This early victory of the princes, which at one stroke created a completely new source of power, as effective in their hands as was the English church in the hands of the Tudors, was consolidated at the end of the century, when the dangers of the Counter-Reformation forced the Protestants to accept a new degree of discipline and subordination. Under the influence of Melanchthon, the fervent spirit of primitive Lutheranism was whittled away; the Formula of Concord of 1577, defining the orthodox Lutheran faith and reducing it to a system, introduced a period of stagnation, in which the reformed faith stood on the defensive. This attitude, imposed by the struggle with the Counter-Reformation, was encouraged by the princes, who had adopted Lutheranism for their own profit, and who, regarding their ecclesiastical supremacy as a branch of their secular and territorial power, naturally favoured the development of rigorous orthodoxy, of uniformity and of discipline. Thus was bred the dull, conservative Lutheranism of the seventeenth century, which allied itself with the territorial powers, and established a rigorous disciplinary system subordinating every individual to a state in which the civil and ecclesiastical authorities reigned in concert. Incorporated in the principalities, Lutheranism became hostile to the idea of national unity, which inspired the early popular and democratic phase of the Reformation: the territorial churches became pillars supporting princely power. Nor was the position in Catholic Germany different. In order to make headway, the Counter-Reformation needed the coercive power of the princes, who thus became the determining factor in ecclesiastical affairs, because without them Catholicism would have been quite unable to maintain itself.

The evolution of Lutheranism towards a system of territorial churches, the subordination of religion to the dictates of the princes, also had a stifling effect on political activity. The Reformation had brought a breath of fresh air into Germany. As all churches, Lutheran, Calvinist and Catholic, in their struggle for power developed rigid canons of orthodoxy, this was lost. The whole weight of the organized churches, including their influence over education and morality, was thrown into the scales on the side of government: they were content to preach the duty of obedience to divinely-appointed authority, inculcating the narrow doctrine that man serves God best by gaining a living for his family, performing his everyday duties and conforming with the authority of the state. Thus, between a family life inspired by an old-fashioned patriarchalism and a state not so much patriarchal as despotic, there was — apart from associations of no political significance — no approved outlet for the energies of the individual, particularly of the middle classes; there was no opportunity for broad political activity, such as might develop the political education of the citizens.[1]

These developments, which exercised durable influence on the mentality of the middle classes, leading inevitably to both religious

---

[1] The significance of the changes in the character of Lutheranism is emphasized particularly by E. Vermeil, *Germany's Three Reichs* (1944), on whose conclusions the above paragraphs are largely based.

and political indifferentism, occurred at a time when, on the political plane, the middle classes were fighting a losing battle. The subordination of the towns to the princes began, we saw,[1] in the fifteenth century. Their economic decline occurred in the main in the sixteenth century. In part it was a corollary of the rise of Polish and Russian power on the Baltic, depriving the German merchants of their eastern markets;[2] in part it was due to the competition of English, Flemish and Scandinavian merchants, supported by their governments.[3] The consequence was a rapid deterioration in the position of the Hanseatic League, which was in full decay by the end of the sixteenth century, and in 1630 only the three cities of Lübeck, Hamburg and Bremen were represented at the Hanseatic diet. The decline of the cities of the south occurred somewhat later: a turning-point was reached when the great Augsburg banking house of Fugger — a house which gave its name to a whole period of history — went under as a result of the repudiation of the Spanish debt in 1627. Both in north and south, the Thirty Years War completed the ruin of the towns, particularly of the imperial cities which could not claim the protection of a territorial prince. Internally, the decline of trade both before and during the wars encouraged the rise of restrictions and monopolies, through which the more powerful elements sought to engross what commerce remained. The result was a spirit of petty egoism, and a general stagnation, which was the counterpart to the political indifferentism and weakness already noted.

The collapse of German commerce under the strain of state-fostered foreign competition and civil war weakened the towns in their relations with the princes and simultaneously deranged the whole balance between princes and estates, since the towns on account of their financial resources had, at the end of the fifteenth century, played a leading part in the activities of the States-General. In the territorial states, only very few cities — Rostock and Wismar, Stralsund and Greifswald are examples — succeeded in maintaining any real measure of independence; the rest sank into direct subordination to the general territorial administration, and lost their autonomy except occasionally for petty matters of police. The magistrates, although still mostly chosen by the citizens or a section of the

---

[1] Above, p. 49.

[2] Ivan III closed the German merchant's gild at Novgorod in 1494.

[3] It is characteristic of Habsburg policy that they favoured their dominions in the Netherlands at the expense of the German merchants.

town, were appointed by the territorial authority, and their activities were so circumscribed by the organs of the central administration that they ceased in practice to be representatives of the community they governed and acted rather as indirectly appointed officials of the state. The only exceptions were in territories where the estates succeeded in maintaining their hold; here the interests of the cities were in some measure secured by their participation in activities of the States-General. But in lands like Austria, or Prussia, or Bavaria, where the princes broke the power of the estates, the cities sank rapidly to the level of mere units or districts in the general scheme of territorial administration.

The decline of the towns was thus one aspect of the wider struggle between the princes and the estates, which broke out almost inevitably as a result of the increase in the power of the princes after the Reformation. Once they had bound the territorial churches to the secular power, the princes sought to drive home their advantage by attacking the nobility and the towns and freeing themselves from dependence on the States-General. In the main this occurred in the seventeenth century, for the most part after the settlement of 1648 — the decline of the Bavarian *Landtag* in the sixteenth century was exceptional — and it was a process which affected Catholic and Protestant states equally. Indeed, the forces of the Counter-Reformation were a powerful instrument for the suppression of the estates and their independence; they were used ruthlessly throughout the Austrian dominions, particularly in Austria itself, where the Catholic rulers broke the backbone of the *Landtag* by persecuting and driving out the Protestant nobility, its most trusty members, at a time when the population of Austria was still almost totally Protestant in faith. A similar policy was pursued in Bohemia, Moravia and Silesia, and outside Austrian territory in Bavaria. Thus a practical example was given of the political value of the victory won by the princes at the Peace of Augsburg in 1555: the famous principle *cuius regio eius religio* was not merely a means of securing religious uniformity, but also an instrument for creating a régime of absolutism.

The uneasy peace of the period between 1555 and 1618 was used by the princes to consolidate their position, and in particular to reorganize and modernize their administrative machinery, which was notoriously retrograde by comparison with England and France. It was at this time that institutions more complex than a single undifferentiated household administration were generally introduced; [1] separate 'colleges' of privy councillors with distinct spheres of action, which were the forerunners of the later ministries, now made their appearance, including consistorial courts controlling all matters of religion. It was at this time that offices like the chancery were detached from the royal court and took up permanent residence in a fixed place. But above all this was the period of the rise of a professional bureaucracy, which became the backbone of princely government, freeing it from dependence on the estates. It was because of the progress of administrative machinery that the princes were able so easily to absorb the autonomous régimes of the towns, and it was with the support of the new bureaucracy, which had every interest in the dissolution of the old aristocratic and oligarchic society, that they broke the power of the States-General.

The struggle between the princes and the estates was fought out over the issue of taxation. In this fundamental question, an effective solution seemed to have been reached by the beginning of the sixteenth century, by which time in practically every territory the prince had secured the right to levy extraordinary taxes with the assent of the States-General, which were thereby accorded a recognized place in German political institutions. Particularly important, from the point of view of the estates, was the control exercised by the States-General over the taxes which it granted. The prince, through his officials, collected and administered the ordinary revenues; but the taxes granted by the estates remained from beginning to end under their control. They passed into the *Landeskasse*, a treasury distinct from the prince's exchequer, were administered by officers responsible to the estates, and a strict watch was maintained to ensure that they were used only for the purposes for which they were granted. In this respect the German States-General had initially even more effective control than the English parliament; there were here all the germs of a sound constitutional development. But the changed situation after the Reformation and after the Thirty Years War, in particular the waning of the middle classes, brought all such development to a standstill. At the very period when in England the Civil Wars and the Whig Revolution assured the predominance of

---

[1] Cf. Andreas, *Deutschland vor der Reformation*, 258-265; there is also a useful essay in Below's *Territorium u. Stadt.* — Most princes imitated Austrian institutions, which were reorganized under Maximilian I and Ferdinand I on Burgundian and French models.

the mercantile classes, in Germany the princes freed themselves from the financial and therewith from all other control by the estates. As we have noted, the process began in the sixteenth century in Bavaria, where dukes William and Ludwig, who ruled jointly after 1514, raised three general taxes without seeking the assent of the estates; and by 1577 the decay had proceeded so far that the Bavarian estates, realizing their own powerlessness, themselves requested that their assemblies should be discontinued. In Prussia, where the position of the estates had been materially strengthened during the period of Polish overlordship, when the Polish crown deliberately lent them its support as a counterpoise to the dukes, the struggle was longer and harder. The nobility stood out for the 'policy of the Fatherland' — i.e. local East Prussian interests — in opposition to the 'despotism of the Mark of Brandenburg', and it was only during the reign of the Great Elector (1640-1688) that their opposition was broken. When in 1653 the nobility accepted an offer of increased rights over the peasantry on their estates, and in exchange granted the Elector the taxes he demanded for a period of six years, a turning point was reached. After the six-year period was ended, the Elector demanded the permanent concession of a regular yearly contribution, and when this was secured in 1662, there was no longer any question of an effective right of assent or dissent by the estates.

These are examples of a process completed almost everywhere in Germany during the generation following the Peace of 1648, if not before. How far the process had gone is illustrated by the fact that in 1670 an attempt was made to introduce an imperial edict of general application throughout the empire, annulling the right of assent to taxation vested in the States-General of the various territories. This attempt to secure an overriding legal ruling was unsuccessful, but as a compromise a general order to all subjects was issued, setting forth their duty to contribute 'in accordance with custom and the princes' needs'. Thus it was established that the princes were within their rights in levying taxes at the rate which had become customary since the introduction of taxation with the assent of the States-General at the end of the fifteenth century. In addition, the princes shook off control by introducing new forms of taxation which lay outside the normal sphere of control of the States-General. It was a more diffi-cult matter to get rid of the separate financial administration of the *Landeskasse*, which remained in existence in Brandenburg-Prussia,

Austria and Bavaria, long after the estates had lost their right of assent to taxation; but with the elimination of the estates' control the difference between the two *Kassen* was gradually reduced to one of historical origin, and the two took their place side by side as two branches of a single administration. In Prussia financial dualism was for all practical purposes eliminated by Frederick William I in 1713.

With the termination of the estates' participation in taxation and the emergence of an unlimited princely right to levy taxes, the foundations of the power of the *Landtage* collapsed. Thereafter few princes experienced difficulty in consolidating an absolutist régime. In the course of the seventeenth century full assemblies of the Estates were mostly replaced by committees, which were easily subjected to the ruler's will, and which (like the French *parlement* two centuries earlier) became little more than formal meetings for registering the sovereign's decisions. Only in Saxony, Brunswick, Hesse, Württemberg and Mecklenburg did the estates succeed in retaining their status, clinging to their inherited rights and privileges with dogged tenacity; but even here they rarely played any active part in public life. Elsewhere they fell into powerlessness, particularly in the three major states, Austria, Prussia and Bavaria, and the organs of absolute government were constructed without their assent or consultation. At most they were left with certain customary rights, which became increasingly insignificant as new forms and methods of government arose; taxation and legislation became prerogatives of the ruler, and supported by a bureaucratic system often built up on the French model and by a mercenary army, the princes emerged from the ruin of the Thirty Years War as absolute rulers.

§ 14. *The Peace of Westphalia* (1648) *and the Sovereignty of the Princes*

The new absolutism received its consecration in the peace of Westphalia. The accretion of power which came to the princes as a result of the ruin of their subjects during the Thirty Years War profoundly modified their relations with the empire, particularly as the Emperor Ferdinand III appeared at the settlement as the defeated party. Their victory over their subjects set them on the road to absolute sovereignty, and made it natural for them to claim sovereignty in the international sphere. Even before the beginning of the war in 1618 a number of the more important states — Hesse, Saxony, Brandenburg and, in particular, the Palatinate — had maintained ambassadors at foreign courts, working side by side with, and as often as not in opposition to, the imperial ambassadors. They had not hesitated to enter into foreign alliances without imperial assent. Hence by 1648 they were already acting as independent powers in European politics, and this independence was increased when in the subsequent fifty years more and more imperial territories fell under princes who were independent kings in virtue of possessions lying outside the boundaries of the empire. This was true, in the first place of Austria which, linked with the Habsburg possessions in Hungary, the Netherlands and Italy, was much more a European power than a German state. It was true of Saxony which, once the leading Protestant state of Germany, saw its elector become a Catholic in order to compass the Polish crown. The elector of Hanover ascended the English throne in 1714. One group of northern provinces was under the king of Sweden, another under the king of Denmark. Even the elector of Brandenburg when, in 1701, he was raised to the royal dignity, took his title from his Prussian lands, which — after existing under Polish overlordship from 1466 to 1657 — were no longer accounted, as in the middle ages, a province of the empire.

This extensive association of German with non-German lands meant in practice a disruption of the territorial unity of Germany, scarcely less final than the annexation of the west German province of Alsace by France which occurred simultaneously. After 1648 the empire had, properly speaking, no history of its own; the territories went their own way without any reference to the destiny of Germany as a whole. In the peace of Westphalia the princes secured all the essentials and most of the trappings of sovereignty; thereafter every prince was emperor in his lands.[1] All the powers they had acquired as a result of the Reformation and of the Thirty Years War were confirmed in the treaty of peace, in particular their authority in matters of religion and their right to form alliances. Any direct interference by the emperor with administration, either in particular regions or throughout the empire, was henceforth out of the question. Even in petty matters like the post, which was an imperial

---

[1] Hence the maxim: 'quilibet status tantum potest in suo territorio, quantum imperator in imperio'.

monopoly, or the granting of patents of nobility, the princes were jealous of the emperor's rights, and sought (mostly successfully) to bring them into their own hands. It was characteristic, again, of the new state of affairs that the Diet of the Empire, although it had long ceased to be an effective organ of government, was in 1663 transformed into a permanent congress of ambassadors, sitting at Regensburg; here again the change emphasized the independence of the princes. It was, however, in the international sphere that the disruption of the empire was most clearly seen. At the Congress of Utrecht in 1713, for example, only envoys of the several states, not of the empire, were present, while in the following year, when peace was concluded with France, two separate treaties were promulgated at an interval of six months: the treaty of Rastatt for the emperor, and the treaty of Baden for the princes. Even the pretence of maintaining the formal unity of the empire had been dropped.

The sovereign rights accorded to the princes in the peace of Westphalia were in theory limited by the rights of the empire. They were supposed to observe the laws of the empire and only deviate from them in cases where imperial law laid no claim to general binding force. They were under the obligation to participate in imperial wars, and were not permitted to remain neutral. Any treaties or alliances they entered into were limited by the stipulation that they must not be directed against the peace of either empire or emperor. These limitations were all so many empty words. In the War of the Spanish Succession, Bavaria did not hesitate to take up arms on the side of France. In the War of the Austrian Succession, the empire as a body took no part. In the Seven Years War Prussia successfully defied the whole might of the empire. In the Wars of the French Revolution, Prussia withdrew independently into neutrality in 1795, Austria in 1797, although so far as the empire as a whole was concerned the war was not concluded until the Peace of Lunéville in 1801. Independent action in the pursuit of independent interests was thus the rule: long before the demise of the empire was publicly announced in 1806, it had ceased to exist. After 1648 it was no longer an empire at all, and scarcely even a federation: it had no common treasury, no efficient common tribunals and no means of coercing a refractory member. The seventeenth-century jurist who described it as an irregular body — 'irregulare aliquod corpus et monstro simile' — was making a plain statement of fact. It was neither a limited monarchy, as imperialist writers vainly sought to prove, nor a federal state, since effective means of federal action were lacking, particularly in the sphere of war and foreign relations. A federal constitution might still have been created in the days of Maximilian I, but everything that had happened between 1520 and 1648 had made a federal solution more remote.

There was not even sufficient identity of interests to constitute a basis for a federation of sovereign states. After the Thirty Years War the cleavage of interests between the Protestant north and the Catholic south was a dominant theme, and the confessional division was organized in such a way as to permit either party, Catholic or Protestant, to paralyse any attempt at action by the Diet. Intent on their own aggrandizement and on the exploitation of their own sovereign powers, not even the greatest of the princes had any vision of German unity or any consciousness of overriding German nationality. After 1648 the empire was a meaningless historical survival, Germany a geographical expression: the reality was embedded in the principalities, whose only ambition was to develop into sovereign monarchies.

§ 15. *Germany and Europe after the Peace of Westphalia*

The full recognition of the sovereignty of the princes, Catholic and Protestant alike, which was contained in the peace of Westphalia affected not only the relations of the princes with the emperor, but also the relations of the empire with foreign powers. The princes might be sovereigns in their own lands, unimpeded either by the emperor above or by the estates below, but – excluding Austria – none, not even Brandenburg-Prussia, was more than a second-rate power, and none was strong enough to adopt an attitude of independence in foreign affairs. In this respect the treaties of 1648, although only registering the completion of a process which was centuries old, marked a fatal decline in Germany's standing in Europe. Austria after 1648, and particularly in the eighteenth century, concentrated its attention increasingly on its interests in Eastern Europe, turning its back on Germany, and the princes were left to fend for themselves. The result showed how illusory their sovereign independence was, when they came face to face with a great power imbued with strong political traditions. France had had its clients among the German princes since the days of Philip Augustus at the end of the twelfth century; but never was French intervention in German politics so open, so continual and so consistent as after 1648. Broken, divided, economically weak, and lacking any sense of national unity, Germany became virtually a French protectorate: even in the imperial diet at Regensburg the dominant voice was that of the French ambassador.

The peace treaties of 1648 themselves gave a formal sanction to French interference at the conclusion of a war in which Austria was defeated by French and Swedish arms. Opposition to Austria threw one party among the princes into the arms of France, and identified their interests with French interests. As far back as 1552 Maurice of Saxony and his Protestant confederates had allied with France, and agreed to the French annexation of Metz, Toul and Verdun, in order to shake off 'the bestial Spanish servitude'; thereafter France was rarely without an organized party in Germany. In 1629 Richelieu drew up the famous memorial, demonstrating the necessity for French intervention in German affairs, which embodied the permanent guiding principles of French policy,[1] and a few months later, in association with Sweden, put them into effect. A weak and disunited Germany was a French interest — was, indeed, perhaps France's major interest in Europe — and it was with this interest to the fore that its representatives went to the peace conference in 1648. After 1629 the Thirty Years War had been a war between the Bourbons and the Habsburgs fought out on German soil, but in the treaties of 1648 it was represented as a struggle for the rights and liberties of the German princes against attempts at their suppression by the Emperor, in which the French king appeared as the protector of German liberties. The fact that the king of France was a party to the treaty made him a guarantor of the constitution which it regulated, and his guardianship became a pretext for a general supervision of German domestic politics. A similar rôle was assigned to Sweden in the north; but the decline of Swedish power, culminating in the defeat of Poltava in 1709, left France alone in the field. The territorial settlement of 1648 was exactly suited to French interests: a Germany divided into 234 territorial units, all claiming sovereign independence and at loggerheads among themselves, had

---

[1] 'I shall play the part which Richelieu assigned to France', Napoleon remarked to a Prussian negotiator. — The first, introductory volume of Sorel's *L'Europe et la révolution française* provides a brilliant sketch of the coherence of French policy through the centuries.

no hope of escaping French tutelage. With good reason a French diplomat later described the peace of Westphalia as 'one of the finest jewels in the French crown'.[1]

Thus the scene was set for Louis XIV, who systematically exploited German internal divisions as a means of securing both the territorial aggrandizement of France at the expense of Germany, and his own predominance in Europe. At the first imperial election under the new régime, in 1658, France solemnly warned the electors that their freedom was passing from them and that the imperial crown was becoming hereditary in one family, and offered to subsidize the elector of Bavaria, if he would become emperor. A considerable party was even in favour of conferring the imperial crown on Louis himself. When, in the end, the Austrian Leopold I was elected France immediately confronted him with an organized opposition party. Led by the archbishop of Mainz, a number of princes formed the Rhenish League, under French direction, for protection against possible encroachments by Austria. Thus Louis XIV set himself up as protector of the states of south and south-western Germany, and from 1679 his domination over Germany was complete. This period saw the French annexation of Strassburg (1681), and the notorious 'reunions', which consolidated French power in Alsace, assured French control of the left bank of the Rhine for a long stretch from the Swiss frontier northwards, and left the imperial territories of Burgundy to the south and Lorraine to the north, at the mercy of France. The latter, after being more than once under French occupation, was finally annexed, with the county of Bar, in 1766, when it had been under continuous French occupation since 1735; the free county of Burgundy was ceded to France at the peace of Rastatt in 1714.

It was no accident that the period immediately following the peace of Westphalia witnessed the most serious territorial losses ever suffered by Germany. Inability to defend the frontiers was the inevitable consequence of the total breakdown of internal cohesion. Only the princes immediately concerned by the French 'rectifications' in Alsace and elsewhere were prepared to fight; the others saw only an opportunity for an 'arrangement' to their own advantage. Austria deliberately sacrificed Alsace in order to gain a free hand in Hungary;

[1] Sorel, op. cit., I, 401. Sorel himself described the treaties characteristically as 'la grande œuvre européenne de l'ancienne France' (op. cit., I, 270).

Brandenburg under the Great Elector, a pensioner of France, deliberately obstructed the formation of an anti-French alliance, when the unprovoked French occupation of Strassburg in 1681 aroused — for almost the last time in the history of the old empire — a wave of resentment and national feeling. It was the opposition of a great European coalition, headed by Great Britain, and not of the German princes, which put a halt to French expansion in the Wars of the Palatinate (1688-1697) and of the Spanish Succession (1701-1714). Only their fear of French hegemony postponed the annexation of the left bank of the Rhine from the age of Louis XIV to that of Napoleon. If the integrity of Germany was maintained, it was because it was in the interests of the powers to prevent the absorption piecemeal of German territory by one of their number; the empire was preserved after 1648 because the great powers could not agree on the division of the spoils.

After 1648 Germany ceased to be a factor in European politics. Only Austria and (after 1748) Prussia counted for anything, and because of their rivalry they tended to cancel each other out. When Frederick the Great in 1756 threw over the traditional Prussian friendship with France in favour of an alliance with England, it was simply the sign for the cementing of a Franco-Austrian alliance. Whatever the constellation of forces, French preponderance over Germany was assured. With France in possession of Alsace and of Strassburg — 'a door through which she can invade German soil as often as she wishes'[1] — western Germany lay exposed and defenceless under the threat of French domination and eventual French conquest, subject without notice to French interference. Because it was a cardinal point of French policy to keep Germany weak and disunited, the long subjection, moral as well as political, of Germany to France was a major cause of German backwardness. A century later, on the eve of the French Revolution, an official of the French foreign ministry described Germany as a bulwark of France which it was an essential French interest to keep in its present state of disunity.[2] Like the papacy in the days of Gregory VII and Innocent

---

[1] When the question of recovering Strassburg after the French occupation of 1681 was under debate, the commander of the imperial army, Margrave Ludwig Wilhelm of Baden-Baden said: 'For Germany the possession of this city means simply a lasting pledge of peace. For France it is a door constantly open for war, through which she can invade German soil as often as she wishes.' Louis XIV's view was substantially the same: Alsace was, he said, 'a passage for our troops to Germany'. Cf. Sorel, op. cit., I, 283-4.

[2] Haller, *France and Germany*, 99.

III, only with a more ruthless logic, France allied with and fostered German particularism in order to further its own political designs. When Napoleon announced that the annihilation of German nationality was an essential feature of his policy, he was only reducing to a phrase what had been the essence of French policy since Riche- lieu. To annex the German territories on the left bank of the Rhine, to dominate the rest by exploiting their divisions, to prevent the growth of common German interests and impede the resurgence of German nationalism, all this was traditional in French policy; but never was it more easily or more successfully encompassed than during the centuries when the principalities, having broken loose and secured sovereignty, assumed control of German destinies. Their concentration on their own interests, their forgetfulness of their common German inheritance, created the atmosphere most congenial to French intrigue: in a welter of petty and divergent interests the princes, for a consideration, gladly signed the death- warrant of Germany.

§ 16. *The Eighteenth Century: Stagnation and Retrogression*

The decay of any sense of common German nationality was a measure of the havoc wrought in Germany by the Wars of Religion and the ordeal of the Thirty Years War. Earlier a spirit of national- ism had flourished despite (and, indeed, in reaction to) political impotence and fragmentation. After 1648 it perished with the dis- memberment of the empire. A last flicker was aroused by the pre- datory schemes of Louis XIV; but it was soon spent, and its political effect was nil. Art and literature both bore witness to the exhaustion of the German spirit, which found its last refuge in the music of Buxte- hude (1637-1707) and Bach (1685-1750). Except for music, where the reverberations of the Reformation still found an echo, the progress of territorialism substituted for the strongly personal and popular art of the Reformation a courtly and aristocratic art aloof from the people and servilely imitative of France and Italy. In this it faithfully reflected political conditions. Nothing more clearly illustrates the extent of the decline which overtook Germany in the seventeenth century than the disappearance of the ideals and impulses which had inspired the generation of 1500-1525.

The disappearance of any sense of common German nationality, which was the mark of the century following the peace of Westphalia, was in part the result of sheer physical exhaustion. The desolation of the Thirty Years War left the country incapable of any great corporate effort, concerned almost exclusively with recovery from material devastation. But it was also the result of the triumph of the princes, which the treaties of 1648 had registered. With the ruin of the peasantry and the middle classes government in the German principalities lost all popular associations and all capacity to appeal to popular loyalty; the petty absolutisms of Germany neither possessed nor sought any foundation or support in the people. This was a cardinal fact in German history throughout this period. The absolutism established by the princes after 1648 had, of course, certain advantages to confer; but divorced as it was from the people, it had neither the power to take root nor the resources to grow and mature. A strong autocratic régime was, all in all, a benefit in the years immediately following the Thirty Years War, when the restoration of peace, order and stable government was a first necessity, and no less valuable was the work of the princes in bringing up to date the organs of administration, without which no régime could begin to cope with the intricate problems of modern government. In restoring an ordered administration after a generation of civil war the princes performed a necessary task. But the benefits conferred were meagre when set against the cost; the triumph of the princes was paid for by the German people.

When the principalities rose to power in the thirteenth century it looked as though they would triumph because they, rather than the empire, were capable of absorbing and giving expression to all the vital elements in German life; when they re-arose at the end of the fifteenth century, it was because the princes had found a means of harnessing to their governments the strong currents of political life which emerged in the fourteenth century. Nothing of the sort could be said of the absolutisms which came into existence after 1648. After the ruin of the middle classes there was no vigorous third estate capable either of controlling or of stimulating government. Not all the princes of the new dispensation were tyrants or despots, but all the governments had this in common, that they served no purpose except their own existence. After 1648 government was an 'end in itself'. It exploited the people, because exploitation was its object; it maintained a routine; it revolved on its own axis; but it made no progress, because it had no objectives outside itself towards which to progress; its ideal was a static society, self-sufficient and quiescent. The result of the long process of German territorial development was thus petrifaction: Germany existed but it did not live.

Every change which we have traced in the history of Germany between 1520 and 1648 played its part in confining German political life within the rigid framework of a petrifying territorial absolutism. In the first place, the two hundred odd states which emerged as the ill-assorted, inconsequential units of German political life after the upheavals of the Thirty Years War, were too small to flourish or to achieve a real measure of self-sufficiency except by a conservatism which closed the door on all that was progressive. Their boundaries, still broken by enclaves and determined by the whims of dynastic accident, corresponded to no reality. They were artificial creations, which were unable to stand on their own feet, and only existed as clients of France or of the opponents of France. The princes who ruled them had no object except to continue to rule, unless it were to make their rule more profitable by adding more acres and more bodies to contribute to taxation. With rare exceptions they still acted largely as landed proprietors, who farmed their patrimony to raise an income to support their households, courts and palaces. Thus the resources of the land, dissipated in small fractions, were wasted on the upkeep of a senseless multiplicity of court establishments which served no useful purpose. When we view palaces like the Zwinger in Dresden or Bruchsal, the residence after 1722 of the prince-bishops of Speyer, with their colonnades and wings and orangeries and pavilions, our admiration should be tempered by the knowledge that they were bought by the sweat of an oppressed peasantry, by the acceptance of subsidies from France, and by the sale of mercenaries to the great powers.[1] It should be tempered also

---

[1] Cf. Rörig, *Ursachen u. Auswirkungen des deutschen Partikularismus* (1937), 28-29: 'The lunatic sums which Karl-Eugen of Württemberg frivolled away on Italian opera, French ballet, etc. led not only to taxation bordering on forced loans, but also to the provision of 6,000 soldiers (in return for corresponding subsidies) to the French for their war against Frederick the Great of Prussia. But the best proposition for princes with easy consciences occurred after 1775, when England was in need of soldiers for the American war. The landgrave of Hesse-Kassel did the best business at this period, because the relatively orderly state of his military arrangements enabled him to deliver better troops than competitors like the Elector of Bavaria or Karl-Eugen of Württemberg. Of 19,400 Hessians supplied to the British government 13,900 returned in 1784; casualties numbered 7,500.'

G

by the knowledge that the object of these establishments was to create an impression of solidity, permanence and magnificence, which was the very opposite of the truth, with the object of magnifying the distance between prince and subjects and holding the latter in political subjection; the prince-bishop of Speyer, in his regal splendour at Bruchsal, did not hesitate to notify his people that 'the commanding will of his majesty is none other than the commanding will of God himself'.

These petty absolutisms, whose sole object was self-glorification, rested on the twin pillars of the administration and the army, with moral support from the church. The Thirty Years War had created a soldiery which the princes took care to retain on a permanent footing after peace was restored. Thus the standing army made its first appearance in Germany as a basis and support for local absolutism; in international politics the independent value of the petty armies of the German princes was negligible, but they were useful for securing stability and obedience at home. Hence all liquid capital available, when the voracious needs of princely pomp had been satisfied, was applied to building up armies and bureaucracies. It was to finance the administration and the military system that more and more rigorous taxation was imposed after 1650, because the administration and the army were the instruments through which the princes reduced their subjects to tutelage. The multiplication of bureaucracies was a mark of the times. It was the natural consequence of territorial fragmentation and patriarchal despotism, and it provided an occupation for the middle classes, which had lost their natural outlet with the decay of commerce. Urban life now revolved round the busy wheels of administration: as the old towns of Germany went down, new towns like Weimar or Karlsruhe, Mannheim or Erlangen, arose whose *raison d'être* was the princely residence to which they were attached and the bureaucracies they housed. For all their beauty they were parasites, draining the country and contributing nothing to its economic resources. Likewise the effects on German middle-class society of its absorption into a bureaucracy inspired by no ideal of public service, were deplorable. The multitude of officials regarded their employment as a particular favour, demanding in return the most absolute subservience to their princely employer. They were in most cases chosen on principle from other territories, so as not to be contaminated by sympathy with the people it was their duty to exploit. And finally their energies were frivolled away in an endlessly repeated administrative routine, in which each territory aped its neighbour: over two hundred states each with its customs system and customs officials, each with its chancery, each with its organization of direct and indirect taxation! The mere cost of this multiplication was sufficient to prevent any recovery of prosperity, to absorb the surpluses which should have gone into commerce and industry, to tie Germany to an obsolescent social and economic system in which agriculture was predominant.

Germany needed a period of peace and stability after the desolation and ravages of the Thirty Years War; but the absolutist régime robbed the country of the benefits of peace and stability. The innumerable territorial barriers alone were a fatal obstacle to commerce. The upkeep of the lavish establishments of the ruling dynasties was a dead weight crushing all productive sections of the population. The very stagnation which the régime produced tended to perpetuate absolutism. Lack of opportunity drove the best elements to seek their fortunes abroad. It was not only that government was divorced from the people; more important was the fact that there were not, as in France or in England, flourishing economic interests which demanded a voice in government. When German territorialism set obstacles in the path of the rise of the middle class, it created a situation which fundamentally differentiated Germany from the west. The cardinal vice of the absolutist régime was that it allowed the middle class to survive only as the salaried pensioner of government. In part, this was deliberate policy, as the sustained attacks on the estates imply. In part, it was the inescapable result of the political conditions under which absolutism rose to power. The mercantilism of the age was not foreign to Germany; there were princes enough who saw the advantage of pursuing a definite economic policy and stimulating economic life; but the units were in general too small and artificial, the bounds within which they worked too narrow, for mercantilism to register any notable success. Except for provinces like Meissen, with its rich mineral deposits, commerce and industry in Germany, ruined in the Thirty Years War, continued to be fragile growths, even where most carefully tended, and the middle classes remained economically and politically weak.

Through absolutism, therefore, Germany was riveted to an agrarian régime, which was harsh and oppressive. Almost the sole productive element in the population was the peasantry, which for that very reason was mercilessly exploited by princes whose expenditure, modelled on the standards of Versailles, created an insatiable demand for revenue. It would be hard to say which was the more characteristic feature of the régime, the decay of the bourgeoisie or the deterioration in the position of the peasantry. In west and south-west Germany, the classical land of the petty principality, where prince and landlord were often one, the depression of the peasantry had begun early, the prince using his public powers to reinforce his hold, as landlord, over the peasant population; while the very fact that most landlords were *rentiers*, who had no interest in the working of the land but only in the rents they got out of it, exposed the tenantry to the worst excesses of rack-renting. It was conditions such as these which provoked the Peasants' Wars of 1524-1525, and it was for this reason that the risings occurred almost exclusively in south-west Germany: their failure and the vicious reaction which followed caused further deterioration. But it was in the states of north and north-east Germany, whose very existence was due to the labours of a prosperous free peasantry, that the most sweeping changes occurred. Here again the beginnings reach back to the end of the middle ages, to the century between 1350 and 1450, when the weakening of government and the alienation of rights and properties by impecunious princes played into the hands of the nobility, who took over by grant or usurpation rights of justice and taxation and the public services which the peasants had owed to the government. Thus they asserted rights over the peasants which they had not possessed in the early days of colonization, and the descendants of the early peasant colonists lost the privileges which had attracted their forefathers to the east, particularly the privilege of direct connexion with government cutting out all intermediate authorities. Thereafter many factors contributed to widen the cleft between the nobility and the peasantry and to bring the latter, shorn of their free status, into subjection to the former. The secularization of Church lands, which fell (as in England) in large part into the hands of the aristocracy, was a major factor in raising the east German Junkers head and shoulders above their peasant neighbours, and in helping them to consolidate their scattered holdings into great estates.[1] In those parts of the Reich which fell temporarily under Polish rule, like Prussia, the peasants were ruined, for Polish law encouraged simultaneously both the most extreme forms of serfdom and the most arrant excesses of aristocratic privilege.[2] Another factor affecting the peasants was the struggle between the princes and the estates, for it was often precisely by compensating the nobility at the expense of the peasants, by recognizing the subjection of the peasantry to the nobility and conferring extensive new rights on the latter, that the princes obtained acquiescence in the destruction of the powers of the *Landtag*.[3] Nor should it be forgotten that the *Landtage*, representing the interests of the privileged classes, were themselves instruments for attacking the rights of the peasantry, and that where the *Landtag* retained its privileges (for example, in Mecklenburg) the depression of the peasantry proceeded most systematically. It was, however, not until the Thirty Years War ruined agriculture that the peasants of north and north-east Germany were finally crushed. They had neither the resources nor the capital for recovery, and after the conclusion of the wars in 1648 the nobility won all along the line. The second half of the seventeenth century saw an extraordinary increase in the number of big noble estates, and the reduction of the peasantry to a state of abject servility.

This was the period when, throughout the north and north-east, peasants were ejected from their holdings to permit the consolidation of demesne farms, when compulsory services (often unlimited in custom or practice) were introduced to compensate for the shortage of labour following the drop in population during the Thirty Years War, when the peasants were reduced to the status of bondmen tied to the glebe. What had begun in consequence of the Thirty Years War was accentuated by the Northern War (1700-1721) and by the Seven Years War (1756-1763). Frederick the Great in Prussia and Joseph II in Austria made some attempt to protect the peasants, if

[1] The position in the middle ages was very different; cf. above, p. 44-5. By contrast von Below (*Territorium u. Stadt*, 48) points to Bavaria, where there was no secularization of church lands and where consequently the scattered holdings of the peasants were a material obstacle to the consolidation of aristocratic estates.

[2] Cf. Treitschke, *Origins of Prussianism* (1942), 150. The expectation of despotic privileges on the Polish model was one of the inducements held out to the Prussian estates to persuade them to desert the Teutonic Order; ibid., 131-2.

[3] For an example of this process at a turning-point in Brandenburg-Prussian history, cf. above, p. 77.

only to ensure that they were not too oppressed to shoulder the burden of taxation or to serve as soldiers; but their success was small, and their policy remained exceptional. In general, government gave the nobility a free hand, unwilling to arouse the hostility of the only element strong enough to oppose it, and desirous of providing for the class on which it still relied for leadership in war. Thus arose the Junker caste and the *Rittergut* of the German east. Dispossessing the peasant owners, the nobility carved out a place for themselves under the aegis of absolutism by consolidating vast estates on which they practised large-scale agriculture; they created a new feudalism more rigorous and repressive than mediaeval Germany had ever known; lording it over a ruined peasantry, they became a dominant power in the land.

The final achievement of the period of absolutism was thus the creation of an agricultural proletariat. The peasants were simply chattels, attached to the estate on which they were born, with no hope of improving either their economic lot or their personal status. Improvements in agricultural technique in the second half of the eighteenth century, although restoring agrarian prosperity, brought them no benefits; indeed, in so far as they contributed to the rise of large-scale capitalist agriculture, they added new hardships to old, in the form of enclosures and loss of commons. The peasants counted for nothing in the state, but on them fell its burdens; while the nobility were exempt from direct taxation, the peasants were left with little more than a third of the money they earned. Impoverishment and stagnation were the result. The nobility made agriculture a paying concern by the merciless extortion of heavy predial services, and thus assured their own position; but for Germany as a whole there was no escape from retrogression. The interests which dominated the principalities were too narrow and too harshly predatory to permit of progress. The rigid class structure, and the lack of intermediate gradations between the privileged few and the disfranchised masses, petrified the social structure. The aristocracy, after its retirement to its estates, where in feudal aloofness it exercised all the attributes of government, thought only of maintaining its privileges by raising barriers against all parvenus; anxiously scrutinizing pedigrees and arranging marriages, it formed itself into a closed caste. At certain princely courts and residences a breath of 'enlightenment' was in the air, but in the country — where, in a patrimonial agrarian society, economic and political power lay — a rigorous, stifling conservatism was the rule. A flourishing middle class, with commercial ties extending far and wide, might have transcended the political fragmentation of Germany; but no breadth of vision was to be expected of the dominant agrarian aristocracy in a country cut into more than two hundred segments.

Thus for a century and more after 1648 Germany stagnated. Petty dynasties, class-bound nobilities and corrupt oligarchies, all guided by narrow motives of self-interest, exercised a harsh and oppressive domination over a peasantry and a middle class both ruined by the Thirty Years War. Initiative and freedom were stifled in the strait-waistcoat of a rigidly stratified society. The only opportunity afforded to the middle class was in the service of the princes; and the only bourgeois element which found any scope within the system was therefore a class-conscious body of civil servants, lawyers, university teachers and professional placemen, who glorified the system which assured their existence. For all others, the very structure of Germany was an incitement to live apart from the bureaucratic machinery through which a petty state bore down on the individual. Associations which might have invigorated social or political life were stifled and discouraged; the legal system with its strong flavour of Roman jurisprudence frowned on them as survivals from a barbarous age, the princes opposed any organization standing between them and the direct exploitation of their subjects. Political life was dead, its place taken by the mechanical clockwork of administration. The narrow ambit of the principalities stultified political activity, while the classes which earlier had looked to wider political horizons beyond the frontiers of the principalities had withered and enervated. Never was the divorce between government and the life of the people so complete. The system with its narrow, dominating aristocratic caste and its repressive feudalism is often thought of and described as an outgrowth of the middle ages, the survival of an out-of-date system accounted for by the retrograde character of German political development. This is at best only partly true. The characteristic features of absolutism, the exacting administration, the dependence on a standing army, the oppressive bondage of the peasantry, even the arrogant isolation of the aristocracy, were all products of the seventeenth and eighteenth centuries, which cannot be paralleled in the middle ages. Mediaeval

German society had been marked by the fluidity and inherent vigour of social classes, the rise and fall of social groups; it had allowed ample play, particularly in the fourteenth century, to free, spontaneous associations which enriched the texture of economic, social and political life; it had drawn its strength from a stalwart, energetic peasantry; it had suffered more from looseness of organization than from rigidity, but had derived the incidental benefits of a loose political structure in the form of vigorous local and regional activities. Far from being incorporated in the principalities, this regional life and local solidarity was stamped out under the dead weight of uniform administrative practices by governments which arbitrarily destroyed older provincial unities at the behest of dynastic interests. The rigidity and stagnation which set in after 1648, the dissociation of the people from the governments set over them, were not the result of the perpetuation of mediaeval conditions, but the symptom of their death. What was tragic in German history, however, was that with the end of mediaeval society nothing living and progressive was found to take its place. The germs of a new society had been there for all to see as late as the reign of Maximilian I (1493-1519). But they were crushed out of existence by the events of the next century and a half, by the entanglements of Habsburg policy, by foreign intervention in German affairs, by religious disunity, and by the long desolation of savage wars. The result was the establishment of the petrifying régime of petty absolutism, which brought neither comfort for the present nor hope for the future.

§ 17. The Rise of Prussia, the French Revolution and the Collapse of the Old Order

The historian's only interest in this stultifying ossification lies in the process by which it was brought to an end, and in its durable effects on the people who underwent it. What the latter were, may (after the foregoing description of the absolutist régime) be summarized under five headings: the fortification of the privileges of a narrow aristocratic caste, more enduringly entrenched even than the absolutist régime itself; the degradation of the agricultural population; the obstacles placed in the way of the liberation and political education of the middle classes; the establishment of the bureaucracy and the army — the officer was simply an official of another order — as the backbone of government; and finally the rigorous stratification of society with each group or class allotted a predetermined place and no scope for individual talent or initiative to overstep the predetermined class divisions. All these characteristics, the results of a century and a half of petty despotism, outlasted the régime under which they were born; they were its lasting consequences, and even in the nineteenth and twentieth centuries they could not be ignored. The absolutist régime itself was more fragile. The political structure of Germany after 1648 was, we have seen, intimately dependent on the European system with which it was integrated. The German *status quo* was ultimately a by-product of the European *status quo*; lacking inherent stability, it had no chance of survival once the European balance of power underwent violent change. The German principalities were simply counters in the game of European politics, too weak in construction to resist outside pressure. Hence, when the end came, it came quickly. Two factors brought about the downfall of the régime of 1648: first, the rise of Prussia, the emergence from the federal body of a state capable (as was proved in the Seven Years War) of standing firm on its own feet, and secondly the upheavals of the years 1789-1815. In the midst of the latter, unmourned and almost unheeded in the revolutions of the Napoleonic period, the old empire, a meaningless survival, finally passed away.

The rise of Brandenburg-Prussia from the ranks of a second-class German territory began when, after the ruin of the Palatinate in the Thirty Years War, it succeeded to the primacy among the German Protestant states. Its early territorial history is a story of tenacity, and the political testaments written by the heads of the house of Hohenzollern for their successors show how meticulously opportunities were foreseen and watched;[1] but the main feature of Hohenzollern policy is a clear, calculating realization that for a German principality to prosper its governing principle must be to exploit the divisions among the great powers. Between Russia, Sweden and Poland, with France in the background, Hohenzollern policy steered a devious but gradually successful course. The peace of Westphalia brought Brandenburg the eastern half of Pomerania, as well as the bishoprics of Magdeburg, Halberstadt, Minden and

---

[1] They were collected and published in two volumes in 1919-1920 by G. Küntzel and M. Hass, *Die politischen Testamente der Hohenzollern*.

Kammin; in 1657 Prussia (which had been in the hands of the
electors of Brandenburg since 1618) was freed from Polish suzerainty; in 1721 at the end of the Northern Wars, the more important
part of western Pomerania, including Stettin, was added at the
expense of Sweden. In the west the Cleves duchies had been acquired
by inheritance in 1614. Thus the scattered Hohenzollern territories,
reaching across north Germany from the Dutch to the Polish

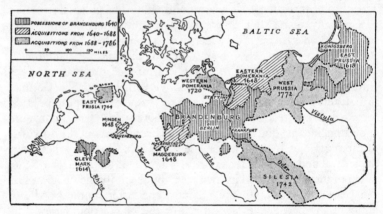

The growth of Brandenburg-Prussia to the end of the reign of
Frederick the Great.

frontiers, fell into three main blocks: the Mark itself with the con-
tiguous Pomeranian lands, the east Prussian duchy, and the smaller
and less consolidated but richer possessions towards the Rhine.
Even minor acquisitions outside these blocks had their importance:
Minden, for example, was a bridge over the Weser and one of the
main points on the great road from east to west connecting Berlin
with the Lower Rhine, Magdeburg was one of the most important
crossings over the Elbe. By the end of the seventeenth century the
Hohenzollern domains were ceasing to be merely a dynastic
agglomeration and beginning to look like the framework of a great
kingdom.

What distinguished the history of Prussia from that of the other
second-class German states in the generations following the peace of
Westphalia was, however, less its territorial history which revealed
no clear signs of future greatness until Frederick the Great launched

his momentous attack on Austria in 1740, than the subordination of all inhabitants, from the king downwards, to the service of the state. This was, in part, a consequence of the wide dispersal of Hohenzollern territory which — contrasted, for example, with Saxony or Bavaria — required special measures to safeguard the scattered fragments, and obtain even a minimum of cohesion. It was also a result of a clear understanding that, to secure any measure of respect and consideration from the greater powers which dominated German politics, a strong military organization was requisite. Provided that the rulers of the Prussian state had the requisite will and traditions and tenacity, the exigencies of their frontiers and the imperative demands of Prussia's critical position in central Europe, directly threatened by major powers like Russia and Sweden and Austria, were a powerful incentive to constructive statesmanship. In the three great rulers who formed Prussia, the Great Elector (1640-1688), Frederick William I (1713-1740) and Frederick the Great (1740-1786), leaders were found who impressed a tradition in keeping with Prussia's geographical and political circumstances.

The detailed story of the reforms and reorganization carried out by the Prussian rulers of the eighteenth century, described again and again by historians seeking the key to the modern history of Germany, can be passed over. What concerns us is the contrast with the history of the rest of Germany in this period. This contrast begins at the top and permeates the whole State; it is perhaps most marked where, in the army and in the administration, similarity seems at first glance most striking. In Prussia, as in the rest of Germany, the administration and the army were fundamental. In the scattered territories stretching from the Rhine to the Vistula, there was no unity of common tradition; there was not, until the end of the eighteenth century, the unity of a common body of law; still less was there any common representative body; the one unity was that of a common administration and a Prussian army. But the Prussian army, unlike the armies of most other states of the period, was not simply a mercenary army. Because of the high cost of recruiting abroad, Frederick William I began to adopt the plan of raising his troops from his own population. By the end of his reign half of his army of 80,000 men was recruited at home; proportionate to the population on which he could call, it was far larger — as well as better drilled and disciplined — than any other army in Europe.[1] Moreover it was maintained, unlike the mercenary armies of the other principalities, which were paid for by foreign subsidies, from the resources of the Prussian state. Frederick William I left, at the end of his reign, a war treasure of six million thalers, equivalent to nearly one and a half years' revenues; Frederick the Great, in spite of his wars, left a treasure of fifty million thalers, amounting to more than two and a quarter years of a revenue which was itself triple the amount that his father had collected. The frugality, the rigorous checks on expenditure, and the careful management which produced this result, were the mark of Prussian administration. Here again there is a marked contrast with the lavish expenditure and the overgrown bureaucracy of the average princely household; practising a severe economy both at court and in the cost of the public administration, the Prussian monarchy disciplined itself to sacrifice the revenues of the crown to the overriding requirements of the state. Brandenburg-Prussia, not the Hohenzollern dynasty, came first: 'I am the Finance Minister and the Field-Marshal of the King of Prussia', said Frederick William I.

It was this sense of subordination to a higher duty, of responsibility to a higher power, which distinguished the Prussian state from the rest of eighteenth-century Germany. The famous doctrine that the prince is the servant of the state was a peculiarly Prussian doctrine. Its kings conscripted the lives of their peasants and the services of their nobles, but they also conscripted themselves. Whatever view we may hold of the ideal of the Fatherland, there can be no doubt whatever that it represented a revolutionary advance over the practice and theory of the other German states, petrifying in obedience to the personal will and arbitrary whims of minor potentates. Whilst they languished under an old-fashioned and wasteful misgovernment, Prussia set the example of an administration which, while rigorously frugal, strove to develop the resources of the land, of a highly-disciplined army, and of a tradition of service which in some degree took the place of free political activity as a source of

[1] The army of Frederick William I stood at 80,000 when the population of his territories was only some 2,000,000; it was 1 in 25 of the population when the army of France was about 1 in 150. By 1789 the regular army of Prussia was 162,000 men, rising in time of war to 250,000, compared with the French army of 173,000, which could be increased in war to 211,000 or (including the militia) to 287,000. At this date the population of Prussia was less than one-third that of France. Cf. E. Barker, *The Development of Public Services in Western Europe, 1660-1930* (1944), 42-43.

cohesion. Under the constant pressure of royal precept and royal example the people of Prussia alone among the people of Germany developed a close relationship with the state. It was a stern relationship, based on duty and obedience, on austerity and work; its substance was the obligation of every individual, low and exalted, rich and poor, to serve the state with body and soul in life and death. But, in contrast with the aimlessness and arbitrariness of political life elsewhere, even this rigorous doctrine of self-abnegation caught hold, and its sterling value was proved in the Seven Years War when the indomitable resistance put up by Frederick the Great in face of an overwhelming combination of the powers was made possible by the solid support and sacrifices of his people. How absolute that support was is illustrated by the fact that, in the county of Ravensburg, soldiers who deserted were denied the benefits of confession and holy communion and refused admittance to their homes.

The rise of Prussia to the rank of a great power modified the whole European constellation, and laid the foundation for the reconstruction of Germany after the French Revolution and the Napoleonic Wars had overthrown the old order and brought about a basic territorial simplification. Its emergence as a European power would have been impossible without the work of internal consolidation to which Frederick William I and Frederick the Great directed their energies, the latter particularly in the decade 1745-1755, following the Treaty of Dresden, and after the conclusion of the Seven Years War when a vast programme of reform was inaugurated to heal the wounds the state had suffered in the struggle. But the driving force behind this consolidation was the unity of the people round the crown under the pressure of war and resistance to external threats. The wars with Austria between 1740 and 1763 at once completed the development of the Prussian state and signalled its arrival in the ranks of the great powers. The Treaty of Huburtusburg, signed on February 15th, 1763, demonstrated that the empire no longer contained one great power only, but two; and of these two Prussia was essentially the German power. Austria was more and more involved in eastern Europe and Italy (in 1736 it had bartered away Lorraine for Tuscany), and had been ready in the Seven Years War to abandon its Belgian provinces to France and east Prussia to Russia in return for support against Prussia. With the loss of Silesia it surrendered to Prussia the predominating position in Germany, and the changed relations of the two powers were seen when, in 1785, Frederick grouped round him the electors of Mainz, Hannover and Saxony and a host of minor states in a League of Princes for defence against the emperor, Joseph II, who was seeking to restore Austrian power and prestige in Germany. The League of Princes was no attempt at a reorganization of the decrepit imperial constitution; its object was simply to maintain the *status quo*, and on this score it was severely criticized by contemporaries;[1] but it certainly reflected and marked the complete redistribution of power within Germany which followed the victory of Prussia in the Seven Years War.

With its powerful standing army and its remarkable financial strength, Prussia after 1763 was well able to stand on its own feet. But it was in no position to assume the leadership of Germany or to free Germany from foreign tutelage. The equilibrium between Austria and Prussia in the second half of the eighteenth century enhanced rather than diminished the influence of foreign powers in German affairs, in the first place that of Russia under Catherine II, who assumed the rôle of arbiter between the two German powers, in the second place the all-pervading influence of France. It was only with the greatest effort that Frederick, in the last years of his reign, contrived to maintain the position he had won for himself and for Prussia, particularly when in 1781 Austria and Russia drew together. It was fear of Russia and open jealousy and distrust between Austria and Prussia which led to the three partitions of Poland in 1772, 1792 and 1795. These partitions (and the acquisition of the margraviate of Ansbach and Bayreuth in 1791) materially added to the territories under Prussian rule; but, apart from the acquisition of West Prussia in 1772 — a territory still essentially German in spite of three centuries of Polish misrule — they were a source of weakness and administrative difficulties, rather than of strength. From the point of view of Prussian interests, the partition of Poland was an ill-conceived policy, which brought nothing but misfortune in its

---

[1] Thus Johannes von Müller, in *Deutschlands Erwartungen vom Fürstenbunde*: 'If the German Union serves for nothing better than to maintain the *status quo*, it is against the eternal order of God, by which neither the physical nor the moral world remains for a moment in the *status quo*, but all is life and motion and progress. To exist without law or justice, without security from arbitrary imposts, doubtful whether we can preserve from day to day our children, our honour, our liberties, our rights, our lives, helpless before superior force, without a beneficial connexion between our states, without a national spirit at all, this is the *status quo* of our nation. And it is this that the Union is meant to maintain.'

train; but its explanation lies less in the pursuit of Prussian interests than in the tension between the three eastern powers. Each feared the aggrandizement of the other; each was determined, in the spirit of the age, to secure 'compensations'; and the two German powers in particular, beneath a cloak of agreement and co-operation, were divided by a fundamental opposition so deep-rooted as to preclude even the idea of combining, with or without Poland, against Russia or in defence of German interests. Neither Prussian policy nor Austrian policy was a German policy; and their crippling hostility, in which each neutralized the other, left the German territories outside the Prussian and Austrian borders a prey to foreign intrigue and foreign intervention. While Frederick William II of Prussia concentrated his efforts on protecting his Polish acquisitions, fearful lest Austria should come to a secret understanding with Russia to rob him of his spoils, a regenerate France, inspired by the fresh vigour of 1789, marched into western Germany, intent on securing at long last the 'natural' frontiers which, since the days of Philip the Fair five centuries earlier, had been the ambition of French policy. France's frontiers, declared Danton at the beginning of 1793, have been fixed by nature on the Rhine: 'it is there that our boundaries are fated to be placed, and no power on earth shall keep us from our goal'.

The resurgence of France, the hostility between Austria and Prussia, and the oblivion of both the great German powers to German interests, combined within little more than a decade to bring about the complete and final collapse of the old order in Germany. After the partition of Poland, in which Austria and Prussia had co-operated with Russia, both turned without hesitation or scruple to a partition of Germany in co-operation with France. Like every earlier protagonist of French expansion since the first beginnings of French chauvinism, Napoleon found willing accomplices within Germany itself. As early as 1793 Frederick William II withdrew his troops from the west, announcing that thenceforward he intended to devote himself exclusively to the interests of Prussia, and in 1795 he made peace with France by the treaty of Basel. From that moment Prussia abandoned all opposition to the annexation by France of the left bank of the Rhine, merely stipulating that the French should assist her to obtain appropriate compensation in Germany for the Prussian territories lost on the Lower Rhine.

Austria resisted more resolutely, taking up arms in 1799 and 1805; but from the time of the peace of Campo Formio in 1797, she also, like Prussia, was ready to adopt a policy of 'compensations',[1] and in the peace of Lunéville (1801) that ominous principle was enshrined.

The deals which followed brought the territorial system of 1648 crashing down. A resolution of the diet on February 25th, 1803, began by suppressing the ecclesiastical principalities, and soon the imperial towns and other small territories suffered the same fate of mediatization. The map of Germany was redrawn, and forty territories took the place of two hundred and thirty-four. The secularization of the ecclesiastical principalities was particularly ominous; for the ecclesiastical princes were the chief supporters of the old order, the most loyal adherents of the empire. In their place arose a small number of medium states — Bavaria and Baden, Württemberg, Nassau and Hesse — which owed their position to Napoleon, and were devoted clients of France. Already in 1804 and 1805, sensing that the old order was past, the emperor Francis II began to style himself 'Hereditary Emperor of Austria'. The real emperor was Napoleon, who had adopted the imperial title in 1804, thus at long last realizing the old French dream of succeeding to the inheritance of Charlemagne. His plan for Germany was masterly in its simplicity: to destroy the empire, to make Prussia and Austria neutralize each other, and to create a screen of small states, dependent on France, strong enough to defend themselves against Austria or Prussia, but not sufficiently strong to pursue a policy of their own. This plan became practical politics in 1806. Bavaria, Württemberg, Baden and several other states, to the number of sixteen in all, repudiated the laws of the empire and announced their secession and the formation of a Confederation of the Rhine under French protection.[2] Simultaneously the French envoy announced to the imperial Diet at Regensburg that Napoleon had consented to become protector of the confederate princes, and no longer recognized the existence of the empire. The constitution of the Confederation of the Rhine took place on July 12th: less than a month later, on August 6th, 1806, Francis II formally abdicated the

[1] She 'indemnified herself with Salzburg and the Inn country for the fact that the German Empire lost the Rhineland' (Haller, *France and Germany*, 94).

[2] After the defeat of Prussia in the war of 1806 and the Peace of Tilsit (1807) all the German states with the exception of Austria and Prussia became members of the Confederation.

imperial crown, laying aside the imperial government and freeing all subjects of the empire — in particular the officials and the members of the imperial judiciary — from their oaths and obligations. Thus perished the first empire after almost eight and a half centuries of existence. Politically, it left no gap, for it had been a nullity since 1648; but with it went the last exiguous bond between the German peoples, the one remaining symbol of German unity. The dissolution of the unity for which the Ottonian dynasty had struggled in times long past — a unity secured in the wake of their triumphs in Italy and the east — was now complete: territorialism and particularism, in league with France, had won the long battle which the princes began when, in league with the papacy, they took up arms against the emperor Henry IV in 1076.

CHAPTER IV

THE NINETEENTH AND TWENTIETH CENTURIES
(1806-1939)

§ 18. *The National Revival and the Vienna Settlement* (1806-1815)

IN 1806 all that remained of the German nation, sacrificed to the exigencies of princely politics, were the tenuous bonds of common kinship, the consciousness of a common past and of achievements won in common, unity of language and — despite the deep-cutting differences of confession — unity of culture, reinforced by an extraordinary unanimity of spirit and of thought. These were not political factors and they had no place in the calculations of politicians and statesmen, except as dangerous manifestations to be circumvented. Among the men in power even the German language was in decay: Frederick William II of Prussia could only express himself haltingly in German, and even the patriot Stein habitually used French in conversing with his family. Nor was the unanimity of thought and spirit identified with any of the existing German states; for artificial creations of Napoleonic policy, like Baden or Hesse, that goes without saying, but even Prussia, whose extraordinary achievements and indomitable spirit in the Seven Years War had won admiration far and wide, forfeited its hold over popular imagination in later decades, as Prussian policy proved unable to rise above a narrow, shameless particularism.[1] Stein's famous manifesto of 1812 expressed better than all else the mood of Germany in the decade between the fall of the old order in 1806 and the establishment of a new order in 1815: 'I have only one Fatherland', he proclaimed, 'and that is Germany ... To Germany alone, and not to any one part of it, I am devoted with all my soul. At this turning-point in history the dynasties are for me a matter of the completest indifference. It is my wish that Germany shall be great and strong, in

---

[1] Cf. the criticism above, p. 100, n. 1. — Nowhere in Germany was there less interest in the problems and traditions of the Reich than in Prussia; cf. A. Berney, 'Reichtradition und Nationalstaatsgedanke (1789-1815)', *Hist. Zeitschr.* CXL (1929), 62.

order to recover and maintain its independence and its nationality in its position between Russia and France: that is the interest of the nation and of the whole of Europe . . . My creed is unity.'

The rebirth of this spirit of German nationalism, which had been strangled by the principalities, was the result of the French Revolution and of the Napoleonic domination of Germany. The revolution of 1789, freeing France from the shackles of the *ancien régime* and producing a mighty resurgence, filled Germany with a consciousness of her existing impotence; the system of princely absolutism was seen for what it was, a crippling handicap holding down the German people. But it was the Napoleonic régime which turned this new sense of hope and exaltation into nationalist channels. When the first French troops entered the Rhinelands in 1792, they were welcomed as liberators and 'neo-Frankish brothers'; everywhere there was the belief that, under the banner of 'Liberty, Equality, Fraternity', a new era of brotherhood was dawning. Disillusion soon followed.[1] When Napoleon reverted to a policy of balance of power, of compacts and arrangements with princes at the expense of peoples, it became evident that the brief initial cosmopolitanism of the men of eighty-nine had been suppressed. When, after the peace of Lunéville, he developed his plans for Germany to the full, no one could fail to see that he was putting into effect, with an inexorable logic of his own, the time-honoured policy of the French monarchy, the nationalist schemes of Philip the Fair, of Richelieu and of Louis XIV. Until 1806, as a result of the Prussian policy of compromise and a strict attention to Prussian interests, northern Germany had escaped the menace of war, and it could be argued that the struggle was simply a phase in the age-long contest between Austria and France, between Habsburg and Bourbon, and that the humbling of Austria and the elimination of the empire was a benefit for Germany. But the Franco-Prussian war of 1806, the catastrophic Prussian defeat at Jena, and the destruction of the Prussian state by the Treaty of Tilsit in 1807, changed all this. Western Germany on the right bank of the Rhine became French, partly by annexation and partly through the creation of vassal states, such as the Kingdom of Westphalia and

---

[1] Already before the end of 1792 the conduct of Custine at Frankfurt caused hostile reactions. 'These republicans', it was said, 'are the brothers of the soldiers of Louis XIV, the ravagers of the Palatinate; Custine is a bandit. The philosophers at Paris charged him to make war on the palaces; instead he makes it on wine-cellars, granaries and cash-boxes.' Cf. E. Bourgeois, *Manuel historique de politique étrangère*, II (1920), 78.

the Grand Duchy of Berg, and French was introduced as the official language from Westphalia to Hamburg.

These were the circumstances which provoked the rebirth of German nationalism. The humiliation and sense of impotence inspired by the political bargaining and the cynical accommodations of 1806 were immediately expressed by Heinrich Luden when, in his *Observations on the Confederation of the Rhine* (1808), he wrote that 'the most vital elements in my mind and heart lie buried beneath the ruins of the German nation'. Almost simultaneously, in the winter of 1807-1808, only six months after the Peace of Tilsit, Fichte delivered the course of lectures, afterwards published as *Addresses to the German Nation*, which were expressly directed to 'the German people in general, setting aside and disregarding all those divisions and distinctions between different sections of one nation caused by the unhappy events of past centuries', with the purpose of arousing 'in the minds and hearts of Germans throughout the country a spirit of determined activity'. But reaction to the Napoleonic régime had begun even earlier. Schiller, who earlier had counted himself fortunate in losing his country and gaining the world in exchange, lived to publish *William Tell* (1804) and the ode *Deutsche Grösse* (1801), the former a symbol of Germany's destiny and both the result of Napoleonic oppression. The same national inspiration lay behind Herder's ode *Germanien*, published after his death in 1803. Of more immediate practical importance, however, was the reaction in Prussia following the catastrophe of 1806 — the programme of administrative, social and military reform, including abolition of peasant serfdom, concession of local administrative autonomy and freedom of enterprise, associated for ever with the names of Scharnhorst, Stein and Hardenberg. Scharnhorst set out to turn the Prussian army into a national army, the embodiment of 'all the moral and physical energies of the nation'. Hardenberg and Stein realized that it was impossible to raise Prussia from the rut into which it had fallen without politically modernizing the state, or to win the support of a population devoted to the patriotic cause and ready for heavy sacrifices without giving them an interest in public affairs.

Yet these reforms, indispensable to the resurrection of Prussia, were resisted tenaciously by the ruling class, headed by Frederick William III himself. Like the emperor Maximilian I three hundred years before him, he had no idea of putting himself at the head of a national movement; like Maximilian, he took refuge in a policy of procrastination and obstruction. The War of Liberation, which flamed up in 1813, was a national and popular movement, into which Frederick William III was unwillingly dragged. The alliance with Russia was forced on him against his will, after General Yorck had concluded the convention of Tauroggen on his own responsibility. The famous proclamation 'To My People', foreshadowing the reconstitution of a German empire by the united action of princes and people, was extorted from him with difficulty. Nor, if the prince who had most to gain by a bold assumption of leadership was hesitant and reluctant to the last, were the other German rulers less timid and aloof. The Austrian emperor was even more conscious than Frederick William III of the dangerous implications of a popular movement sweeping Germany, while the king of Württemberg, who had basked so long in Napoleon's favour, did not hesitate to express his indignation at the 'ridiculous notion' of trying to make a 'so-called national unit' out of the multifarious German peoples. Even in the year 1813 — often described as an *annus mirabilis* of German history — when the spirit of national devotion and sacrifice reached heights unparalleled for centuries, the cleft carved by history between the nation and the principalities, between the princes and the people, gaped wide.

It is thus not surprising that the War of Liberation ended without any solution of the German problem. Germany was liberated from French rule and domination; but it was not liberated from the heritage of its own past. It was an ominous foreshadowing of the shape of things to come when Frederick William III's call to his people, issued at Kalisch on March 25th, 1813, was followed before the end of the same year by treaties guaranteeing full sovereignty to Bavaria and Württemberg. A few months later, in the Treaty of Paris (1814), the powers laid down that Germany should be formed into a federation of independent sovereign states, and a year later this principle, decided over the heads of the people, was embodied in the final act of the Congress of Vienna. Apart from changes of detail, the territorial system created by Napoleon in 1806 was accepted as the basis of the new order — a system which, as has been seen, was designed in the interests of French policy to consecrate for ever the sovereignty of the principalities and the territorial divisions of Germany. But these principalities, hitherto united only in and through the Napoleonic empire, of which all but Austria and Prussia were satellites, were now united 'for the maintenance of external and internal security' in the Germanic Confederation. This confederation was, however, a union not of the German people, but of the German states. The federal diet was a meeting of representatives of the governments, and all attempts to secure representation for the people were a failure. As far as the statesmen who produced the settlement were concerned, the national movement which culminated in the War of Liberation might never have occurred. For them the people were still simply the population, to be disposed of in the interests and for the benefit of their lords. How little they had learnt or forgotten was demonstrated by the territorial settlement of the Saar question in the first Peace of Paris: as a whole the Saar was left in French hands, but it was decided to separate a total of 69,000 'souls', divided with minute exactitude into five portions of 13,800 each, as 'compensation' for the princely houses of Mecklenburg-Strelitz, Pappenheim, Saxe-Coburg, Hessen-Homburg and Oldenburg. Such was the recognition which the German people received for its share in the overthrow of Napoleon.

As in earlier centuries, the fate of Germany was settled, its frontiers drawn, by the princes in league with foreign powers. In this respect also the system of 1815 was a direct continuation of the old system. Like the settlement of 1648 the German settlement of 1815 was part of a European settlement: it was drawn up partly in the interests of the German princes, largely in the interests of the great powers, and not at all in the interests of the German people. Thus it was the English desire for a strong barrier against French aggression, reinforced by the necessity for finding territorial compensations to offset the Russian absorption of nearly the whole of Poland, which led to the acquisition by Prussia of a major accretion of territory on the Rhine — a cardinal change in the political geography of the Prussian state and in the direction of Prussian policy without which its rise to predominance between 1815 and 1871 would scarcely have been thinkable. The fall of Napoleon, the defeat of France, brought about a change of masters, but not a change in the system by which the political organization of Germany was made to subserve the interests of the powers. If England, in the person of Castlereagh, set up Prussia as watchdog on the Rhine,

Austria, which was now only in small degree a German state, was interested in the maintenance of the Napoleonic states of south Germany both as a barrier against France and as potential allies against Prussia. Every interest was heard and respected except the interest of the German people. Even the centuries' old plea for a common coinage and for the abolition of barriers to trade and communications – pleas which had been loud as far back as the reform movement of the fifteenth century – were ignored: nothing, in the view of the Congress of Vienna, must stand in the way of the full sovereign prerogatives of the individual German states.

Such, then, was the state of Germany on the threshold of the nineteenth century. The particularism which reached its culmination in 1806 was consecrated and legitimized in 1815; it had carried all before it, and the particular interests of Prussia and Bavaria, of Saxony and Württemberg and the rest, had written the name of Germany off the political map of Europe. On the other hand, none of these states, not even Prussia, had succeeded in taking over, even within the limits of its own territorial boundaries, the loyalties which had formerly animated the Reich; they had existed, most of them, as independent political units since 1648, but none had established that identity of government and people, of state and folk, which gives endurance and stability to political society. They were still, at the end as at the beginning, the arbitrary product of accidental contingencies, superimposed on the population regardless of race, geography or history; they were able to interfere with the economic and social life of the people – and had, in fact, cruelly impeded its healthy development – but they were unable to gather the life of the people round them, to make themselves the centres of popular life and activity, expressing the common interests of their inhabitants. They had, for more than a century after 1648, undermined the sense of common German nationality which had been vigorous as late as the sixteenth century, but they had failed to set anything else in its place. And even that piece of destruction, which for long seemed permanent, proved transitory. The generation between 1790 and 1815 witnessed a revival of the German national spirit so strong that neither the settlement of 1815 nor the repressive régime which followed, was able to expunge it. Furthermore, this nationalism, born of the rancour engendered by French rule and French political domination and inspired by the consciousness of a great German past, transcended the accredited system of particularist sovereignties, and looked beyond the existing states, none of which fulfilled its aspirations, to a new Germany representative of the German people.[1]

§ 19. *Liberalism and National Unity* (1815-1871)

The settlement of 1815 set the stage for the political struggles of the nineteenth century. Already in 1815 a clear-sighted observer, surveying the balance established between Austria and Prussia, remarked that the 'settlement must inevitably lead to a struggle for supremacy in Germany'; but the fundamental issue at stake was less the struggle for supremacy between Austria and Prussia than that between the principles of unity and particularism. What Prussia set out under Bismarck to overcome in the wars of 1866 and 1870 was the particularism enshrined in the Peace of Vienna; and its blows were directed at Austria, and then at France, as the two mainstays of German particularism, the two powers which had organized German territorial disunity in their own interests and to further their own ends. But Prussian policy under Bismarck was designed to further Prussian, not German, interests and to safeguard Prussia's position as a great power; and it was only Bismarck's success that gave general credence to the theory that Prussian self-preservation and the cause of German unity were identical.[2] The Austro-Prussian antithesis was long dormant, strictly subordinated both by

[1] This spirit was well expressed in a letter addressed in 1813 to the future historian, Johann Friedrich Böhmer, by his father in an attempt to dissuade Böhmer from volunteering for service against the French. 'Unhappily', he wrote 'those fighting for the great patriotic cause are not so much Germans as Bavarians, Württemberger, Hessians, Saxons, Nassauer, Würzburger and even subjects of the petty state of Ysenburg. What our fortunes are under so many paltry sovereigns bitter experience has taught us. In this respect, it seems to me that enough is being done for the German princes, but nothing for the people. It is my heartfelt conviction that the latter can only achieve happiness and well-being, if Germany constitutes one great Reich . . . To this end no sacrifices would be too great, but so far this objective has not been set before us' (Berney, op. cit., 67).

[2] Bismarck himself in his later life and writings propagated the theory that he had planned from the beginning to unite Germany, and the official historians of the Hohenzollern empire, in particular Treitschke and Sybel, set themselves the task of proving that Prussia had always been the nucleus of a united Germany and had aimed at unification consistently since 1815. Already before 1918, however, German historians (e.g. Friedrich Meinecke and Erich Brandenburg) had discredited the forced interpretations of Treitschke (*Deutsche Geschichte im 19. Jahrhundert*, Engl. trans. 1915-1919) and Sybel (*Die Begründung des deutschen Reiches*, Engl. trans. 1890-1891), and after 1918 a more critical attitude towards their views, hitherto long predominant, became general.

Metternich and by Frederick William III to princely solidarity against popular unrest and radical and nationalist agitation; but even when it emerged into the open, far from expressing in practical terms the problem of unity or particularism, the struggle between Austria and Prussia cut across that issue. At the time of the War of Liberation Fichte had sought to identify the cause of Prussia and German unity, but in the generation down to 1848 the overwhelming majority in the politically articulate classes looked to Austria, rather than Prussia, to provide the nucleus of a united German state. On the other hand, the strength of Austria's position in the day-to-day manœuvres of German politics lay in the support of the rulers of the small and medium states, who feared Prussian hegemony, and hoped with Austrian support to resist the movement for unification of which they would necessarily be the first victims. Hence the adherents of Austria comprised irreconcilable elements: conservatives intent only on maintaining the old order, and liberals bent on its destruction. And similar divergencies divided the adherents of Prussia; for where Fichte had envisaged the absorption of Prussia into Germany, a second school of thought (of which Niebuhr was protagonist) postulated the absorption of Germany into Prussia, a solution abhorrent to most liberals. Finally, there was a cleavage between liberalism and nationalism, in so far as many middle-class liberals, satisfied with conditions in the smaller states of southern and western Germany, which had undergone a process of administrative reform under French rule, were opposed to any change which, by destroying the identity of the principalities, might undermine the constitutional régime they enjoyed.

These extreme divergencies of aim exerted decisive influence after 1815. It was because of the disunity and still more the incompatibility of the various groups opposed to the Vienna settlement that the question of national unity was, under the influence of Metternich, so easily dismissed from the field of practical politics. There was no natural alignment between the movement for German unification and existing political forces, and so the movement could not make use of existing political combinations to help it forward. Nor could it, like the radical movement in nineteenth-century England, make use of rapid social and economic change. Germany in 1815 was still almost entirely an agricultural country with old-established handicrafts, such as the weaving of Silesia and the cutlery of Solingen, but without flourishing industries or a prosperous manufacturing class; and although in the next thirty years there was a rise in population amounting to no less than 38 per cent, the proportions of town and country dwellers remained virtually unchanged.[1] Few towns had recovered from the effects of the Thirty Years War and the stagnation of the eighteenth century, and at the beginning of the nineteenth century the total population of all the free cities and university towns of Germany was scarcely the equivalent of the population of Paris. Hence neither industrial capitalists nor industrial workers existed as a serious political force, and the towns were still, as in the eighteenth century, dominated by a professional and bureaucratic middle class, which had little to gain by radical political change. These factors go far to explain the failure of the revolution of 1848-1849; but what is more remarkable is the persistence in such circumstances of a current of radical and national feeling strong enough, once the European situation was favourable, to kindle the sparks of revolution. As soon as the outbreak of revolution in France created the necessary external conditions, a spontaneous uprising against which the princely governments were helpless, took place simultaneously throughout the thirty-nine German states; and in this movement the old problem of national unity and particularism quickly came to the fore. It came to the fore inevitably because ever since the time of Stein it had been manifest that abrogation of the rights of the princes, and of the privileges of the aristocracy which were vested in the principalities, was the first necessary step towards securing the welfare of the German people: no reform was possible, no extension of civil rights, without a thorough revision of the federal system which, from the time of the Carlsbad Decrees (1819), had consistently been applied for the repression of civic liberties.

The attitude of disparagement and contempt once adopted by historians towards the revolution of 1848 — an attitude derived from implicit acceptance of Bismarck's famous judgement: 'The great questions of the day will be settled not by resolutions and majorities — that was the mistake of 1848 and 1849 — but by blood and iron' —

[1] Excluding the Austrian lands, population rose from 24,500,000 in 1816 to 34,000,000 in 1846. But whereas in Prussia 73.5 per cent of the population was classed as rural in 1816, no less than 72 per cent was similarly classified in 1846, and the rural population was still 71.5 per cent of the whole as late as 1852; cf. J. H. Clapham, *The Economic Development of France and Germany, 1815-1914* (1921), 82 sqq.

has given way to a more realistic appraisal of the facts, in which the positive achievements of the movement, and not merely its failure, receive due emphasis.[1] No one doubts that the decisive factor in the failure of the revolution was the unwillingness of the liberals who controlled the Frankfurt parliament to attempt a transformation of 'real power-relations', to offer a social programme such as made the French revolutionary changes of 1789-1793 irrevocable. They strained too anxiously after legality, had too implicit a faith in constitutional schemes unaccompanied by changes in the seat of political power necessary to make them effective; they feared popular upheaval and hoped rather by the creation of a complicated machinery of checks and balances to reform the old order. With no independent power of their own, they were unable to oppose reaction, and as soon as the Prussian armies had reasserted control in Berlin, the fate of the movement was in the hands of the king of Prussia. With Prussian co-operation German unity was possible; without it there was no means of compelling the princes to accept the Frankfurt constitution. By 1849 this hard fact was understood, and a deputation was sent to offer the German crown (Austria excluded) to Frederick William IV. Frederick William's refusal to 'pick up a crown from the gutter' set the seal of defeat on the movement. A radical minority sought, too late, to stir up popular support, but Prussian arms easily suppressed popular risings in Saxony, the Bavarian Palatinate and Baden; and these risings, in any case, failed to secure the support of the liberal majority. On May 28th, 1849, sixty-five members quitted the Frankfurt assembly in a body, declaring that they were not prepared to foster civil war, and would therefore transfer the work of constitutional reform to the governments of the individual states, leaving the national cause to develop of itself. This was abdication, for the prospect of voluntary reforms within the principalities was negligible. The reformers had paid the penalty for their refusal to enlist popular support, to seize the 'victorious moment', and to stimulate a genuine social revolution. And yet it may be doubted, having regard to the backwardness of German social and economic development in 1848, whether a genuine attempt to 'go with the masses' offered any real prospect of success; in which case the failure of the Frankfurt parliament was due

[1] Cf. the useful summary by J. A. Hawgood, 'The Frankfurt Parliament of 1848-1849', in *History*, XVII (1932).

rather to circumstances beyond its control than to the deficiencies of its members and the dilatoriness of its procedure.[1] Economic and political conditions very different from those in France and England, were scarcely favourable to an assertion of middle-class, still less of working-class, power. The important fact about the revolution was therefore the very fact of revolution, of a true popular upheaval sweeping the whole of Germany. The movement of 1848-1849 proved with all finality that the issue of German unity was alive and could not be shelved. Despite all manœuvres under Austrian influence after 1850 to set the clock back, despite the restoration of the old Confederation in its old form, there was in fact no going back on the substantial results of 1848. The ideas and projects of 1848 dominated the mind of the next generation. How firm a hold they had taken was immediately evident when, in 1849, immediately after the triumph of conservative reaction in Prussia, Frederick William IV's minister, Radowitz, took up the ideas of the Frankfurt Assembly and, adapting them to Prussian interests, sought on the basis of the Frankfurt constitution to create a new federation embodying the essential points sought a few weeks earlier by the Frankfurt parliament when it offered the German crown to the king of Prussia. Radowitz's scheme, opposed by Austria and Russia, was no more successful than the Frankfurt programme; but its adoption was an important indication that the ideas of 1848-1849 had come to stay, and it is significant that Bismarck approved Radowitz's policy and believed the opportunity favourable to Prussia. What Radowitz failed to do in 1850, Bismarck achieved in 1867; it was no accident that his North German Constitution of 1867 was in numerous places reminiscent of that of 1849. His debt to the work of 1848-1849, which cleared the road for Prussian action, was greater than he would have liked to admit. Nor, on the other hand, were the 'Fundamental Rights of the German People' — the *Grundrechte* formulated in 1848 — so ineffectual as has been supposed. It was easy for the Federal Diet in 1851 to decree them out of existence; but they remained as a practical statement of radical aims, and no sober minister could doubt the necessity of taking them into account. Here again Bismarck, most realistic and most far-seeing

[1] So much may be said in criticism of Marx and Engels, *Revolution and Counter-Revolution in Germany* (1852) and of the Marxian arguments in Lassalle's *Ueber Verfassungswesen*; otherwise these are still the best analyses of the events of 1848.

statesman of his age, paid an unconscious tribute to the work of 1848-
1849; he did not make the mistake of underestimating the strength
of German liberalism. On the contrary, his very efforts to preserve
the predominance of the Junker aristocracy in Prussia, and in
particular the methods by which he pursued this inflexible objective,
revealed his awareness of the seriousness of the inroads which the
revolution of 1848-1849 had made upon the Junker position. On the
surface, all was as before; but the revolution had failed primarily
because it could not rely on the support of any existing political
force, and if such support were forthcoming he well knew that it
would be fatal both to Prussia's position in Germany and to the
survival in Prussia of the military monarchy and of the Junker caste.
When after 1861, Austria under Schmerling, the leader of the
Austrian party at Frankfurt in 1848, reverted to a liberal policy, and
began to press for a reform of the German confederation, and when
in 1863 the Austrian emperor actually summoned all the German
sovereigns to a congress at Frankfurt to establish a strengthened
federal authority, the only way out for Prussia was war, and Bismarck spent the next three years in diplomatic and military prepara-
tion for the decisive struggle with Austria which broke out in
1866.

Bismarck thus realized that, despite the setback of 1848-1849, German liberalism and nationalism supported by Austria were still a serious threat to Prussian particularism and Prussian aristocratic privilege.
To maintain the prerogatives of the Junker class a conservative
alliance between Austria and Prussia against liberalism was necessary, such as had existed before 1848; against an alliance between
Austria and the German nationalist movement, on the other hand,
Prussia could only hold its own by enlisting the support of the whole
Prussian people, and this implied a surrender to liberalism which
would cut the roots of Junker power. In these circumstances Bismarck sought for long to obtain a conservative alliance with Austria;
but it was a sign of his superb realism that, when this failed, he
grasped the necessity for compromise on one score or the other
with the forces of 1848. Inevitably it was the movement for
national unity with which he came to terms. Liberalism was fatal
to the social order for which Bismarck stood; but nationalism, carefully handled, could be made to subserve the purposes of Prussia.
Thus Bismarck defeated the forces of 1848 by a policy of *divide et*

impera. He separated German national aspirations from the liberal background which, from 1813 to 1848 and in centuries past, had given them meaning. Nationalism had grown strong as an instrument of liberal reform, as an essential means of breaking the stranglehold of particularist interests over the German people; Bismarck's achievement — an achievement which served only the purposes of the Prussian Junker class — was to make it an end in itself and turn it against its liberal past. In Bismarck's system nationalism, long the concomitant of liberalism, was deliberately fostered as an antidote to liberal and radical demands; he offered the German people unity, but at the expense of the radical reform which alone made unity worth while.

Bismarck's accession to power in 1862 was therefore a turning-point in the history of nineteenth-century Germany; his forceful personality, and still more his strategic mastery and firm grasp of political reality, brought into play a totally new approach to the age-old problem of German unity. The German leaders in 1848 had sought liberal reform and national unity, the latter primarily as a means to self-government; Bismarck was not interested in self-government and his approach was therefore different. The basis of his work was the revolutionary ferment of 1848-1849, firstly, because the revolution had made the question of unity an issue which could not be shelved and, secondly, because the projects of Schmerling, to which Bismarck's policy was a hostile reply, were an adaptation of the projects of the Frankfurt parliamentarians. But his methods were new and the foundations on which he built were utterly different. It was not simply that he, unlike the men of 1848, understood the virtues of 'blood and iron' and the futility of 'resolutions and majorities'; rather the contrast was that, pursuing objectives radically different from those of Bismarck, the leaders of the movement of 1848-1849 were not, whereas Bismarck was, prepared to make 'blood and iron' the basis of policy. Bismarck's aim — once he had given up hope of a renewed 'Holy Alliance' with Austria — was to achieve German unity without revolution so as to fend off the social consequences of successful revolution. For this task a firm grasp of the grim realities of power-politics, which the leaders in 1848 had disastrously neglected, was essential both in internal and in foreign relations. In 1848 revolution in Paris and Vienna had momentarily obviated the risk of foreign interference in Germany, and it was one of the tragedies of the failure that the politicians at Frankfurt were incapable of exploiting this unique opportunity to settle Germany's problems without foreign intervention; for in more normal circumstances not only France and Austria but Russia also had a direct interest in maintaining German backwardness and disunity. Hence there was small prospect except in times of revolution – and revolution was the last thing Bismarck wanted – of establishing German unity unless a favourable constellation of forces in Europe had previously been secured. For this reason Bismarck's energies were largely devoted to foreign affairs. The detail of this work may be ignored, although its importance was great. Its keystone was the convention of 1863 with Russia, which acquiesced in Prussian plans in order, with Prussian support, to recover control over the Black Sea which it had lost after the Crimean War. Further stages were the exploitation of differences over Italy to divide Austria and France, and of French projects for the annexation of Belgium to divide France and England. Thus the possibility of the formation of a conservative *bloc* was obviated. Bismarck was fortunate also in having an unwilling accomplice in Louis Napoleon, whose inept and puerile diplomacy played into the Prussian minister's hands.[1] Without doubt, Bismarck's skilful manipulation of the European balance of power was the very foundation of Prussia's military successes against Austria in 1866 and against France in 1870; and these military successes were indispensable steps in the creation of German unity. Louis Napoleon had been prepared, for a moment, to support the formation of a major north German state around Prussia, provided France obtained 'compensations'; but this was a personal policy, for which he failed to secure French support, and in any case it did not extend to a union between Prussia and the German states south of the Main. The exclusion of Austria from Germany, and therewith the end of the crippling Austro-Prussian dualism which reached back to 1763, was a first step; but German unity could not be secured without the defeat of France, the age-old protagonist of German particularism. It was no accident that the defeat of France, the inveterate enemy of German union, and the birth of a united Germany went together, and that the second

[1] For the detail of European diplomacy between 1862 and 1870, which cannot be considered here, cf. A. Debidour, *Histoire diplomatique de l'Europe*, II (1891), 248-401, and R. H. Lord, *The Origins of the War of 1870* (1924).

German empire was proclaimed by the victor at Versailles on January 18th, 1871, sixty-five years after the dissolution of the old empire at the hands of Napoleon Bonaparte.

Many years before 1871 the Prussian militarist, Clausewitz, had ventured the opinion that there was 'only one way for Germany to attain political unity, and that is by the sword: one of the states must bring all others into subjection'. The wars of 1866 and 1870 seemed to prove him right. In many respects it is true that Germany was a Prussian conquest won at the expense of Austria and France. In 1866 German opinion as a whole was on the side of Austria, and even in Prussia, particularly in the Rhinelands, there was resistance to the war, including demonstrations in Berlin. In the Federal Diet all states not absolutely dominated by Prussian guns voted in condemnation of Prussia; and although this vote expressed primarily the opinion of the princes, it also represented liberal middle-class sentiment, which was alienated by Bismarck's unconstitutional government. There is therefore much truth in the view that Germany was 'conquered, not united'. And yet this is not the whole truth. Many long-standing factors worked in Prussia's favour, and it has been said with some justification that 'Germany was practically united before Bismarck began to work at all'.[1] Avoiding the mistakes of 1848-1849, Bismarck built his policy on the firm foundation of existing tendencies, making the most of the factors favourable to the Prussian cause. First among these was the fact that Austria was on the defensive, seeking to check Prussian ambitions, but unwilling herself to shoulder the burdens and responsibilities of German affairs; she was not a competitor herself for the German crown, which Francis I had refused in 1815, but only an opponent determined that the throne the Habsburgs had vacated in 1806 should remain vacant. Secondly, there was the territorial redistribution of Prussian power in the 1815 settlement: stretching from the Rhine to the Vistula, with considerable accretions of territory and a reformed and reinvigorated administration, she was in a position for the first time to close the gap between east and west and dominate the whole of the north German plain. But neither of these advantages was so important as the advent of the industrial revolution, which gave Germany both an overriding practical motive and the means for unification, which had earlier been wanting. The *Zollverein* of 1834,

[1] W. O. Henderson, 'The Zollverein', *History*, XIX (1934), 18.

the modelling of a unifying railway system and the German industrial revolution which began after 1850, were milestones along the
road to the Bismarckian empire of 1871.[1]   They enhanced the sense
of German unity,[2] and both in that respect and as practical instruments of policy they were adroitly used by Prussia, which was
fortunate in possessing the great coalfields of the Ruhr. When after
1850 these deposits were seriously exploited, they provided the
foundation for an iron and steel industry which soon challenged the
old-established industry of Bohemia. The result was that Prussia
made rapid strides forward, quickly out-distancing Austria, which
still remained predominantly rural in structure. Moreover, the
prosperity between 1850 and 1871 greatly favoured Bismarck's
policy. Just as in England after the Great Exhibition of 1851 the
working-class movement entered on a generation of apathy, so in
Germany the dawning of an age of plenty took the sting out of
radical agitation; it seemed in both countries as though well-being
and liberalism would be achieved by the blind working of beneficent
economic forces, broadening from precedent to precedent, and that
the radicalism of 1830-1848 had been no less misguided than unsuccessful. Thus a favourable economic environment made it more easy
for Bismarck to dissociate nationalism from liberalism; the economic
advantages of unification became more evident at the very moment
when the benefits of prosperity made radical reform less urgent.
This was an important point. Bismarck knew full well that, in
opposition to Austria and France, German unity would have to be
conquered; but in relation to the German people he wanted more
than the victory of a conqueror, for only so could victory be made
permanent. He realized as fully as the men of 1848-1849 the gulf
between the national aspirations of 1790-1815 and the reality of the
1815 régime, and he spared no effort to enlist the disappointed hopes
of the German people on the side of Prussia. That he succeeded was

[1] The British expert, Dr. John Bowring, who visited Germany on behalf of the Foreign
Office in 1840, reported that 'the general feeling in Germany towards the *Zollverein* is that
it is the first step towards what is called the Germanization of the people. It has broken down
some of the strongest holds of alienation and hostility. By a community of interests on commercial and trading questions it has prepared the way for a political nationality — it has subdued much local feeling and habit and replaced them by a wider and stronger element of
German nationality' (Henderson, loc. cit.).
[2] As early as 1828 Goethe wrote: 'I have no misgivings about the union of Germany; our
good roads and future railways will do their share'. For railway development cf. Clapham,
op. cit., 150 sqq. Hence Keynes' famous dictum: 'the German Empire was built more truly
on coal and iron than on blood and iron'.

I

due not least of all to the brief phase of prosperity during which his main work was accomplished. National unity without liberal reform would have satisfied no party before 1849, and it was no satisfaction to the German people later after the slump of 1873; but Bismarck had the advantage of circumstances and the skill to use his advantage. When, in 1866, after his victory over Austria, the Prussian parliament indemnified him by 230 votes to 75 for the unconstitutional collection of taxes without parliamentary assent since 1862, it was his first victory over liberalism, the first proof that — for a moment — national unity was rated higher than the benefits of self-government. This victory was driven home in the war with France. Exploiting the follies of Louis Napoleon, Bismarck united the German people, conscious of centuries of French aggression and countless humiliations, under Prussian leadership against France. He acted in the nick of time. Two years later, in 1873, the onset of economic depression again made social and economic problems more acute than national unity; but in the meantime the new order, of which the North German Confederation of 1867 had created the framework, was anchored fast in the constitution of 1871. That constitution set the seal on Bismarck's work.

The establishment of German unity, implicit in the sweeping revolutionary movement of 1848 and thereafter overpoweringly fostered by rapid economic change, was inevitable. What Bismarck did was to determine the particular form which it took, and the particular moment at which it occurred. His masterly diplomacy defeated the inveterate hostility of France, which might otherwise have postponed a decision for decades, and secured with a minimum of upheaval a result which might otherwise have necessitated European war and even revolution. His manipulation of the unitary forces within Germany, on the other hand, ensured that Germany should be united under Prussia. The Prussian solution of the German problem was anything but inevitable; without Bismarck the unification of Germany might well have been accomplished against both the Prussian monarchy and the Prussian aristocracy. Hostility towards Prussia and fear of Prussian hegemony had been lively in 1848; and it was due to Bismarck alone, aided by social and economic developments which he put to good use, that after 1866 this hostility was overcome. The new Reich of 1871 — whatever the theory — was in practice a Prussian Reich, shaped to accord with Prussian interests, constructed in conformity with Prussian traditions, ruled by the dynasty of Hohenzollern, and dominated by the Prussian Junker class. We may admire the steadfast logic with which Bismarck pursued his objects to the very end, the skill with which he triumphed over obstacles which had defeated generations of German statesmen, until the German nation — which in 1806 had been visible only in a transcendental unity of language and of culture — was united in a single political body; but the fact remains that the curse of German particularism was expunged only by the triumph of the most successful of German particularisms, which had no intention of disowning its own particular origins and traditions.

This was made evident by the constitution drawn up for the new empire by Bismarck in 1871. It is usual, in analysing the constitution of 1871, to emphasize its federal character, pointing out that it betrays in every paragraph the conflicts of a thousand years of German history.[1] But the reality was otherwise. The federal rights retained by the states south of the Main, Bavaria in particular, were illusory, and such compromise as Bismarck sanctioned stopped short at a point which debarred them from an effective voice in imperial affairs. In the Federal Council, or Bundesrat, composed of representatives of the constituent states, Prussia had sufficient votes to veto constitutional change, but more important was the fact that the Chancellor was under no necessity of consulting the council on any question of major political importance: during the crisis preceding the outbreak of war in 1914, for example, neither the Bundesrat nor the Reichstag was consulted, and on August 4th both the German people and the federal states were confronted with a *fait accompli*. The abrogation of particularism would, indeed, have been unexceptionable if it had meant the transfer of political power, in the spirit of 1848, from the princes to the people. But such was not the case.[2] There was no mention in the new constitution of the 'Fundamental rights of the German people', on which the Frankfurt parliament of 1848-1849 had spent so much time and toil. The system contrived in 1871 included a Reichstag elected by universal and

[1] Cf. Bryce, *Holy Roman Empire* (ed. 1910), 476 sqq.; A. L. Lowell, *Governments and Parties in Continental Europe*, I (1896), 232 sqq.; F. A. Ogg, *The Governments of Europe* (1919), 202 sqq.; H. Finer, *The Theory and Practice of Modern Government*, I (1932), 258 sqq.; J. A. Hawgood, *Modern Constitutions since 1789* (1939), 238 sqq.

[2] The position was tersely summarized by Laband (*Das Staatsrecht des deutschen Reiches*, I, 91) when he described the empire as 'composed not of 56,000,000 but of 25 members', i.e. the twenty-five member-states of the confederation; cf. Ogg, op. cit., 204.

equal franchise; but its powers were nugatory. It could debate but not initiate legislation; it could in theory control expenditure, but it had no power of voting or refusing to vote taxes — the only effective means of exercising its theoretical control — since the imperial revenue was provided partly from permanent fixed duties, partly by *pro rata* contributions from the individual federal states. In Prussia, however, which had by far the largest population and therefore the heaviest responsibility in imperial finance, representation in the Diet was determined not, as in the Reichstag, by an equal franchise, but by the notorious three-class electoral system, which ensured permanent Junker domination.[1] Finally, the Reichstag had no control over the executive ministers, who were responsible only to the Prussian king who was also German emperor; it might vote against the Chancellor, but only loss of the emperor's confidence, not an adverse vote, entailed his resignation. The German labour leader, Wilhelm Liebknecht, was therefore not wide of the mark in dubbing the Reichstag 'the fig-leaf of absolutism'; the system of government established in 1871 was, in fact, a veiled form of monarchical absolutism vested in the king of Prussia. But beneath this monarchical exterior, decked out with the trappings of representative democracy and federal balance, was the hard reality of the Junker class which — far more effectively than the Hohenzollern monarchy — exercised political influence through the Prussian Diet, wielded economic power through its control of the soil, and dominated imperial policy through its grip over the army and the bureaucracy. The real power of the state was wielded by the Prussian aristocracy: through Bismarck it became the dominant force not only in Prussian but also in German life. The constitution of 1871, fending off the realities of popular self-government, ensured both the preponderance of the Junkers in Prussia and the preponderance of Prussia in the Reich.

§ 20. *The Hohenzollern Empire* (1871-1918)

Bismarck's successes transcended but did not solve the great problems ventilated in 1848. With something of the skill of a gamester he had finessed the strong cards in his opponents' hands,

[1] In the elections for the Prussian Diet in 1908 no less than 600,000 votes were required to secure the return of six Social Democrat deputies, but 418,000 votes were sufficient to gain 212 Conservative seats.

bluffed his way against the insistent demand for radical reform, and saddled Germany with a constitution deliberately designed to conserve the reactionary privileges of a narrow aristocratic caste. It was a momentous fact that, due to Bismarck, Germany passed over into the new age of industrial and capitalist imperialism, which opened after 1871, shackled by its past as embodied in the new constitution. In the first place, the settlement of 1871, although it marked the end of the worst excesses of German particularism, in particular its nefarious tendency to ally with foreign powers,[1] failed to eradicate particularist tendencies; rather these took on a new lease of life in a new constitutional form, securing a measure of genuine popular support hitherto unknown as the expression of the resistance of the people in the more liberal states, particularly Bavaria and Baden, to the Prussian spirit which henceforward dominated the government of the Reich. But more important still was the fact that Bismarck's constitution left intact and even consecrated the vested interests which had grown up with and profited from particularism; indeed, their conservation was the price inexorably extorted by Bismarck for the merging of Germany into one national state. Although Germany in 1871 secured unity, it was not a unity expressed in self-government by the German people; the new state was designed not to represent the will of the German people but to maintain, as in generations past, the subjection of the people to the will of a privileged minority.

It was another question whether Bismarck's settlement of 1871 would stand fast as a barrier against the insistent demand for improved working-conditions, the sweeping away of class pre-rogatives and the introduction of self-government. Bismarck had hoped that it would mark a halting-place, introducing a phase of quiet consolidation; but in fact the new uniformity of administra-tion, the abrogation of internal tariff barriers and the removal of trade restrictions, which followed on unification, inaugurated a period of rapid development in all facets of German life which could not be confined within the rigid structure of the new empire. In

[1] After 1871 there was no revival of the connexion between German particularism and foreign states, which had been so dangerous a factor in German politics in earlier generations; nor was there, either in 1918 or in 1945, any spontaneous movement of separatism. The 'autonomous Government' set up in the Rhine-Palatinate after 1918 by 'an insignificant group of renegades' owed its existence entirely to French intrigue, and collapsed as soon as France — under British pressure — withdrew its support; cf. W. O. Henderson, History, XXVI (1941), 63.

the economic sphere, in particular, the progress of industrialization was stupendous; and the rapid growth of an industrial working-class resulted, as always, in a parallel increase in the political consciousness of the masses. Bismarck's work, far from ending the German revolution, as he intended, released forces beyond his control. The balance he had contrived worked satisfactorily so long as the favourable economic environment in which the new Reich was born, persisted. But the slump of 1873 was a first warning of the precariousness of the balance; and within a few months, as is well known, Bismarck himself lost faith in the stability of his system and began the feverish but hopeless task of erecting new props to hold it up. In the first place, he sought to broaden the basis of the system by admitting the upper middle classes, in particular the great industrialists, to the inner circle of privilege. This alliance was facilitated by the economic depression, which made the industrialists willing to pay the necessary price for governmental support; the instrument by which it was achieved was the Protective Tariff of 1879, in exchange for which the most powerful and influential section of the liberal party entered the government *bloc*. The agrarian tariffs introduced simultaneously won over the smaller farmers and the peasantry, hitherto — in opposition to the Junker landowners — steadfastly liberal. Thus Bismarck contrived to carry on and with the support of a parliamentary majority to launch an attack on the working classes, which — in consequence of the abdication of the liberals — constituted the only force in Germany with a practical and vital interest in the attainment of democracy. It was a two-sided attack. In the first place the Social Democratic party, only founded in 1875, and the free Trade Union movement, only legalized in 1869, were outlawed by anti-Socialist legislation in 1878; the party organization was proscribed, its newspapers suppressed and hundreds of leading members thrown into prison. In the second place, Bismarck sought to take the sting out of labour agitation by the introduction of extensive schemes of social security; between 1883 and 1889 compulsory insurance for workers against sickness, accident, old age, etc. was introduced in the hope of bribing the working classes into quiescence. Neither repression nor cajolery was a success. Organized labour realized that it owed the benefits of Bismarck's social legislation ultimately to the Social Democrat party and its political pressure; and the party continued to grow. Even at the Reichstag elections of 1884, in the heat of the conflict, the Social Democrats increased their vote. The elections of 1890 proved the bankruptcy of Bismarck's system. Twelve years of persecution resulted in a doubling of the Social Democrat vote, which rose to one and a half millions, and an increase in the number of labour members from twelve to thirty-five. Trades Union membership increased similarly from around 50,000 in 1877 to 278,000 in 1891. The election of 1890 was almost a landslide. The right-wing coalition dropped from 220 to 135; the opposition rose from 141 to 207. Bismarck had exhausted all expedients and knew one remedy alone: to abrogate the constitution, to limit the franchise and to drive the Social Democrats completely out of existence. It was a counsel of desperation, involving serious danger of revolution and civil war, and the new emperor, William II, who had succeeded to the throne in 1888, was not prepared to imperil his dynasty in such a gamble. In March 1890 Bismarck was dismissed.

The fall of Bismarck revealed with dramatic abruptness the rising social tension within the Reich; it showed that the forces and ideals of 1848 could not so easily be circumvented as Bismarck had once believed. But it was after Bismarck's fall, during the four years of the 'New Course' between 1890 and 1894, that the intensity of social antagonisms and the inherent instability of the Bismarckian Reich became fully manifest. William II — optimistically underestimating the strength of the opposition — hoped, by sacrificing Bismarck, to conciliate the German people without genuine concessions to radicalism. But Caprivi, who followed Bismarck as chancellor, was a man of undoubted good will, genuinely desirous of following a more liberal course. In foreign affairs he refused to renew the alliance with Russia, which was the symbol of Germany's alignment with the forces of reaction, and sought instead to reach understanding with France and England. In the same spirit he set up in the eastern provinces of Prussia an administration which was favourable to the Polish element in the population, thereby offending both the Czar and the Prussian Junker class, and modified Bismarck's protective system in the interests of the industrial workers, hoping as a result of good relations with England and France to import foodstuffs from abroad instead of subsidizing German agriculture. The corollary of this liberal economic policy and of co-operation with western European liberalism was liberalism at home. In the first place, Caprivi refused to renew Bismarck's anti-socialist laws, with the result that the Social Democrat vote again increased in 1892. Secondly, he proposed to reduce military service from three to two years, and cut the period of the army grant from seven to five years — a token of his rejection of the militarism of 'blood and iron'. Finally, by resigning the Prussian premiership he severed the connexion of the Reich government and Prussia which had been the basis of Bismarck's system, with the intention of reducing Prussia to an equality with the other states and eliminating the Prussian predominance in Germany by which the whole organization of German political life had been perverted. Without doubt Caprivi's progressive policy offered the only prospect of a peaceful evolution of German political life. But it immediately awakened the violent opposition of all classes and factions which had seen in Bismarck's policy a guarantee of their interests; and the constitution of 1871, so long as it remained in force, assured their preponderance in the state. The opposition centred round the question of Prussia. Caprivi's liberalism, his refusal to continue the attack on Social Democracy and his commercial policy, were repugnant to the powerful industrialists; but it was the agrarian interests east of the Elbe which he really injured. In 1894 he came into open conflict with the prime minister of Prussia, who had the solid backing of the Junker class. The only effective remedy would have been far-reaching constitutional change, above all else the transformation of Prussia into a democratic state by the abolition of the iniquitous three-class franchise; but such a course which would have implied revolutionary upheaval, was impossible against the emperor — of whom the chancellor was, according to the constitution of 1871, the servant — and Caprivi never contemplated it. Yet under the constitution of 1871 it was impossible to rule against Prussian opposition, and the breach with Prussia therefore meant stalemate. At the end of 1894 Caprivi passed into oblivion.

If the fall of Bismarck in 1890 was due fundamentally to the strength of German radicalism, over which he had attempted to ride roughshod, the fall of Caprivi in 1894 was due to the strength of German reaction. Taken together, the two events were a revelation of the deadlock in which Germany had been placed by the settlement of 1871. So long as the growing popular forces were excluded from government, there could be no stability for the Reich. But so long as political and social power remained in the hands of the old order, there was no hope of peaceful evolution; for the privileged classes resisted any alteration of the constitution of 1871, which was their charter of privileges, for fear that the flood-waters of radicalism, bursting through the breach, would tear down the whole dam. Moreover, Bismarck's tactical success in 1879 in winning over the liberal industrialists, heightened the tension; for it meant that the liberal middle classes which elsewhere — for example, in England — were driven by their impelling interests to assume leadership in the fight for political democracy, in Germany sided with the forces of reaction. Unlike the British labour movement, which, after the period of Chartism, never had to fight for political democracy, but simply stepped into the liberal inheritance, the German labour movement had to concentrate all its energies on the struggle for democracy; and this struggle was a fight not within but against the existing constitution, which was deliberately designed to place power in the hands of a privileged minority. By allying with heavy industry, Bismarck increased a hundredfold the powers of resistance of this minority. Alone, the Junkers could scarcely have held out more than a few years longer; in alliance with the industrialists their power was practically unchallengeable. And yet in another sense Bismarck's tactical success resulted inevitably in a weakening of Junker predominance. In the coalition with the rising industrialists who controlled the sinews of economic power, the needy Junker landlords could not hope to hold their own; they retained their social prerogatives and their control of the army, but as well-paid servants of the capitalist classes, into whose hands after 1879 the effective government of the Reich passed by rapid stages. After 1890, still more after 1894, German policy was the policy of the industrial and commercial capitalists who exploited their position in the coalition to use the coercive power of government to hold the working classes in check, to destroy competition and to secure markets abroad. In this way Germany was launched along the road of capitalist imperialism. Much against his will, Bismarck was forced between 1884 and 1890 to join with Great Britain and France in the scramble for territories in Africa[1] — a development

---

[1] He resisted the pressure of commercial and financial interests from 1876 to 1884, saying that 'for Germany to acquire colonies would be like a poverty-stricken Polish nobleman providing himself with silks and sables when he needed shirts'. In fact the colonies acquired were useless for emigration and their exploitation was expensive and uneconomical; as late as 1914

which contributed, a decade later, to the demand for a great navy and from 1900 to the naval competition with Great Britain. Still more important, however, was the pressure of the industrialists on the government to find an outlet for the products of heavy industry. The result was the beginning of a phase of economic warfare which, in conflict with rival imperialisms, culminated in the outbreak of European war in 1914.

The development of the European crisis from 1894 to 1914 is a process which we can do no more than illustrate.[1] In Germany, as elsewhere, it was quickened by the simultaneous growth of internal tension; indeed, it is scarcely an exaggeration to state that it was largely accidental whether the attempt to save the old order would take the form of a frontal attack on the forces of democracy at home or of a successful war which, by opening new markets and destroying foreign competition, would reaffirm the stability of the existing system in the face of internal unrest. All parties in all countries were aware that internal and foreign affairs were but two aspects of one and the same problem; hence in all countries organized labour was before 1914 the protagonist of pacifism and internationalism against the self-styled 'national' parties. But of no organized party in Europe was this more true than of the German Social Democrats, for the simple reason that in no country west of the Vistula had the working classes more to lose from a successful imperialistic war. After the fall of Caprivi in 1894 the foundation of brute force on which Junker-industrialist power rested, and the impossibility of compromise were manifest, and it was evident that only a social revolution could shake the existing system. But, as Engels pointed

the area of 1,026,220 square miles acquired by Germany (as against 4,754,000 square miles acquired by England and 3,583,580 square miles acquired by France at the same period) contained only about 5,000 permanent German inhabitants. As the Social Democrats never ceased to point out, the only people who benefited from the colonies were the capitalists; but the large profits which the trading companies made were paid for many times over by the German tax-payers, who had to foot the bill for the subsidies by which the colonies were kept going. Cf. W. O. Henderson, 'The German Colonial Empire, 1884-1918', *History*, XX (1935), 151-158.

[1] There are good, trustworthy accounts in J. A. Spender, *Fifty Years of Europe* (1933), E. Brandenburg, *From Bismarck to the World War* (1930), A. F. Pribram, *England and the International Policy of the European Great Powers, 1871-1914* (1931), G. Lowes Dickinson, *The International Anarchy, 1904-1914* (1937), S. B. Fay, *The Origins of the World War* (1929). Particularly valuable are the various writings of G. P. Gooch; his *History of Modern Europe, 1878-1919* (1923), suffers from having been written before many of the documentary sources had been published, but it has been supplemented and revised in a number of volumes of important essays (*Before the War, Recent Revelations of European Diplomacy*, 1930, etc.), which are marked by exceptional sobriety of judgement; cf. especially the essay on 'Franco-German Relations, 1871-1914', *Studies in Diplomacy and Statecraft* (1942), 1-59.

out in 1895, the development of military technique — in particular the invention of the machine-gun — had destroyed all prospect of successful revolutionary upheaval against loyal troops. Hence the only hope of introducing democracy lay in the shattering of the existing system by its own inherent contradictions. These contradictions were more developed in Germany than elsewhere, except perhaps in Russia. The privileges enjoyed by the Junkers were of a type which had been swept away in France in 1789 and had scarcely existed in England even before the seventeenth-century revolution. The power of the industrialists, on the other hand, was built on unstable foundations; for German heavy industry, because it arrived late on the scene, was a top-heavy structure, extremely sensitive to economic trends and unable to maintain itself without lavish government support. So long as capitalist expansion was maintained and economic prosperity grew, it was possible to placate the working classes and to circumvent political demands by concessions to popular interests, in particular by concessions to the trades unions on questions of hours and wages. But, on the one hand, such a policy only postponed the day of reckoning, for organized labour was not weaned from radicalism by such methods — on the contrary, the Social Democratic party continued to grow, rising by 1903 to 3,000,000 out of a total of 9,000,000 voters. On the other hand, the knowledge that they were swimming against a flood, which would burst its banks at the first moment the wheels of the capitalist machine slowed down, drove the parties in possession to adopt ever more violent methods of maintaining expansion, leading to conflict and acute tension in the field of foreign politics. Even this tension, however, served its purpose in so far as it could be used to divert the attention of the German people from the enemy at home to the enemy abroad. Hence, in line with parallel interests in England and France, German industrialists and conservatives began to organize and finance 'patriotic' societies — the Pan-German League, the Colonial Society, the Navy League — in order both to create a fictitious 'national' solidarity against the foe without and to justify ever-expanding armaments programmes, without which industry could no longer pay its way. Between 1909 and 1914 the cost of British armaments increased by more than 30 per cent, of Russian armaments by 53 per cent, of German armaments by 69 per cent, while the cost of French armaments soared to no less than 86 per cent above the earlier figure. The 'defence' expenditure of the six European great powers, which in 1883 had totalled £140,000,000, reached in 1913 the figure of £404,000,000.

After the fall of Caprivi in 1894 all the tendencies outlined above — in particular the tendency to turn to foreign adventure as a distraction from the insoluble problems of internal politics — gained the upper hand. The tension was such that no statesman could control it, and in fact no statesman made the attempt; they were satisfied if only they could open valves to let off some of the pressure. In these circumstances policy gave place to an endless series of expedients and manœuvres, lacking either principle or coherence, with no object except to maintain as long as possible the actual distribution of power and postpone the dissolution of the existing régime. On the one side, it was essential, if necessary by renewed concessions, to keep the support of the Junkers and industrialists who had demonstrated in their victory over Caprivi the impossibility, under the existing system, of governing without their support. On the other side, since it was clear that the forces in possession would tolerate no step towards self-government, the German people had somehow to be reconciled to the autocratic régime. It was an impossible task, but it was the task assigned — after the brief interlude of Hohenlohe, whose policy amounted only to undoing what Caprivi had done — to Eulenburg and Bülow, who became Secretary of State in 1897 and Chancellor in 1901. To follow the detail of their policy, or that of Bülow's successor, Bethmann-Hollweg, who became Chancellor in 1909, is neither possible nor necessary, for the die was already cast in 1894. The bankruptcy of imperial policy thereafter was implicit in Eulenburg's own definition of his aims: 'to satisfy Germany without injuring the Emperor'. Since the satisfaction which Germany desired was the transformation of imperial autocracy into popular self-government and the destruction of the privileges of the Junker class on which the emperor's power rested, this was a policy of reconciling irreconcilables. In fact, the attempt at reconciliation was only superficial. All the substantial concessions went to the Junkers and industrialists — to the former tax rebates and credits and the new tariff of 1902, to the latter the naval programme of 1900 and the consequent government contracts — and to Bülow was left the task of fobbing off the people by a demonstrative foreign policy, designed to secure solidarity and submission with the cry: 'the fatherland in danger'. But Bülow's foreign policy, the ineptitude of which is proverbial,[1] failed in its purpose. The Morocco crisis of 1905–1906 was followed immediately by a defeat of the military estimates in the Reichstag; the famous incident of the Kaiser's *Daily Telegraph* interview in 1908, in which he painted a totally false picture of the strength of anti-British sentiment in Germany, provoked such a storm that William II had to announce that, in future, he would cease meddling in foreign affairs, and 'respect his constitutional obligations'. But the culmination was reached when, after the second Morocco crisis in 1911, the general elections of 1912 resulted in an outstanding victory for the Social Democrats — the party which throughout had steadfastly refused to vote for the army and navy estimates — which with 4,250,000 votes became the largest single party in the Reichstag. More important, perhaps, was the fact that the middle-class parties at last made up their minds to co-operate with the Social Democrats. The crisis was brought to a head in the following year by the famous Zabern affair, in which the whole country united in protest against Prussian militarism. When the commander of the garrison in this petty Alsatian town arrested and imprisoned some of the inhabitants in defiance of the law, his exhibition of military arrogance stirred all Germany. The chancellor, Bethmann-Hollweg, although convinced that the military were in the wrong, attempted to defend them in the Reichstag. When he was defeated by a vote of 293 to 54, the fig-leaf attached by Bismarck fell off and the nakedness of the power on which government depended, was exposed. Bethmann remained chancellor, the military commander at Zabern was even acquitted by court-martial; but the sole reason was because under the existing constitution there was no means of giving effect to the will of the German people. The Zabern affair, following on the Social Democratic victory in 1912, left no doubt of the seriousness of the crisis within Germany; the long-postponed day of judgement was near.

It is important not to underrate the connexion between the Social Democratic victory in 1912, the Zabern crisis in 1913 and the outbreak of European war in 1914. The sweeping tide of Social Democracy, the growing revolt against internal conditions, profoundly

[1] Cf. Haller, *France and Germany* (1932), 252, 255, 259, 263, summarizing the views of his earlier work, *Die Aera Bülow* (1922).

alarmed the ruling classes in Germany; and there is little room for doubt that one reason why, in the words of a competent French authority, 'the German military aristocracy decided in July 1914 to run the risk of a great European war' was 'a growing sense of discomfort under the increasing pressure of Social Democracy, and a surmise that a bold attempt to give a set-back to Socialism, by asserting themselves once more as the party of war and victory, might prove the wisest course'.[1] Such a calculation — no doubt less conscious than implicitly fostered by the threatening atmosphere — was, of course, not operative by itself; it has to be considered in connexion with the international situation, and with the desire of the German militarists to forestall Franco-Russian preparations for war, which (as was well known among the European cabinets) were timed to mature in 1915.[2] In international affairs the decisive factor was the situation in the Balkans, where Russia, 'having stolen a march on Austria through the success of the Balkan League',[3] had changed the balance of power, and was preparing, after the conclusion of the Second Balkan war in 1913, further alterations in her own favour. Such changes, aimed directly at Austria, were an indirect blow at Germany, which, as the German Foreign Secretary pointed out in an able exposition of the German point of view written in July 1914,[4] could not passively watch 'the establishment of absolute Russian hegemony in the Balkans'. Nevertheless the growing tension in south-east Europe, and the Russian threat to German political and commercial interests in this area, is not alone a sufficient explanation of the drift towards war, and its outbreak in August 1914. During the Balkan wars in 1912-1913 Germany had exercised a strong restraining influence over Austria under considerable provocation, although militarily Austro-German prospects were good; in 1905-1906 at the time of the first Morocco crisis, and in 1908 during the crisis over

---

[1] Cf. E. Halévy, *The World Crisis of 1914-1918* (1930), 11. — This attitude was not, of course, confined to Germany; for England cf. Halévy, *History of the English People 1895-1914*, I, 259, and E. Wingfield-Stretton, *The Victorian Aftermath*, 310 ('if the war peril from Germany delayed much longer to materialize, it seemed quite on the cards that it might be forestalled by revolution. As the Edwardian passes into the Georgian age ... class rises against class ... faction against faction — it is a question whether international will not be anticipated by civil war').

[2] Cf. the report of the conversation of the Serbian minister in London with the French ambassador in December 1911, printed in Lowes Dickinson, op. cit., 214.

[3] R. C. K. Ensor, *England, 1870-1914* (1936), 573; cf. ibid., 463 sqq.

[4] *Die deutschen Dokumente zum Kriegsausbruch* (ed. in collaboration with K. Kautsky by Graf Max Montgelas and Prof. W. Schücking), I (1919), 99-101 (no. 72); cf. Lowes Dickinson, op. cit., 413-5.

Bosnia-Herzegovina, when Russia was suffering from revolution and defeat at the hands of Japan, the prospects of the central powers were brighter still. If the German imperial government which, for all its threats, had no serious intention of provoking war during these earlier crises, was prepared in 1914 to risk a general conflagration, it was not least of all because the internal situation was by this time such that it could not afford even the appearance of a diplomatic setback, which would have condemned it in the eyes of its 'nationalist' supporters and strengthened the opposition. What impelled it along the road of greater risks after 1912 was the situation at home. Bethmann had, after the Social Democrat victory, undertaken to reform the Prussian franchise — the bone of internal discord — but only with the idea of gaining time. In these circumstances any further failure was bound to have disastrous repercussions, and it is significant that in the important dispatch referred to above, the German Foreign Secretary urged the necessity of supporting Austria against Russia 'both for internal and external reasons'. Even in 1914, of course, there was no deliberate intention of provoking European war. Gambling in part on the equivocal attitude of Great Britain, the German government hoped — as all imperialisms hope in such circumstances — for a diplomatic success to justify it in the eyes of the people. It is no part of our task to explain why this was impossible; one factor was without doubt the intense naval rivalry with Great Britain, which cemented the alliance between England, France and Russia. The outcome was that during July 1914, Europe — betrayed by contrary councils and conflicting interests in all the European capitals — broke up into two armed camps and drifted into war.

All historians who have examined the evidence in detail are agreed that responsibility for the outbreak of war in 1914 cannot be placed exclusively on the shoulders of any one government; there was none which was not willing at that stage to use war in the last resort as an instrument of national policy. We have done no more than consider one or two of the factors which affected the calculations of the German government; to trace the development of the crisis in its European ramifications, it would be necessary to do likewise for the other governments involved, which were all beset in greater or lesser degree by the same problems as the ministers of William II. It must also be observed that the factors at play were in their very nature factors influencing the governments and not the peoples; just as the British government desisted from taking parliament into its confidence until August 3rd, by which time the die was cast, so the German government, as has already been noted,[1] sedulously avoided consulting either the Bundesrat or the Reichstag. The result was that war was sprung upon an opinion unprepared, after many false alarms, for the reality of war; and in all countries the people, succumbing to nationalist propaganda, rallied to the nationalist cause against the foe without. In Germany this volte-face was facilitated by the fact that the war was represented as a struggle for the defence of civilization against Czarist despotism, against 'the dark Asiatic power' which (as Marx had said) lay 'in the background as a last resource against the advancing tide of working-class democracy'. In the Social Democrat declaration of August 4th, 1914, announcing the party's majority decision to vote for the war credits, the emphasis lay on the danger of 'a victory of Russian despotism which has soiled itself with the blood of the best of its own people'; compared with the barbarism of Russian Czardom, Hohenzollern absolutism was, for the German worker, the lesser evil. It was a difficult decision — far more difficult than that facing the democratic forces in England and France which had at any rate a clear-cut issue between parliamentary and absolutist imperialism — and it is not easy, reviewing the circumstances, to condemn it out of hand. Nevertheless it ultimately split the Social Democratic party. More important, the German workers' recovery from the initial war fever was rapid; they soon realized that a victory for Hohenzollern imperialism would be scarcely less disastrous for them than defeat by France and Russia. Hence, in spite of ruthless repression, the anti-war movement gained ground more quickly in Germany than elsewhere. Already in March 1915 more than a quarter of the Social Democrats in the Reichstag refused to vote for the war credits, and a few weeks later, in June 1915, an open letter signed by nearly a thousand well-known members of the Social Democratic party denounced the war policy of the majority. At the same period, Karl Liebknecht issued his famous leaflet with the title: 'The Main Enemy Stands at Home'. A year later, on June 17th, 1916, the labour representation in the Prussian diet put forward a motion which, after indicting the German government, went on to declare:—

---

[1] Above, p. 121.

We do not see our well-being in the creation of an imperialist Greater Germany, or of a Mitteleuropa, but in mutual political and economic relations between the nations, fostered by the extension of democracy, the abolition of secret diplomacy and by agreements aiming at the abolition of customs barriers. As international Social Democrats, faithful to our principles, we will never take responsibility for the infringement of the political and economic independence of other nations or for their oppression. For we feel the sufferings of the workers of the countries confronting us to-day as enemies as deeply as we feel the sufferings of our own people. ... The common people of no country have willed the war. ... If the governments of the belligerent countries still refuse to make peace, they act in antagonism to the great masses of the population who long to return to peaceful work. ... We demand that the German government, before all other governments, should take the first step and should relinquish their plans of conquest, thus paving the way for peace. The war and its course have stigmatized the imperialist system of force before the eyes of the world. Peace and civilization cannot be secured by the force of bayonets, by conquest and oppression, but only by the solidarity of the workers of all countries.

This was the authentic voice of the German people; and the fact that it was raised in 1916, more than a year before the entry of the United States into the war, at a time when Germany's armies stood firm in France and Russia, is itself sufficient to disprove the ill-considered assertion that the growing demonstrations against the policy of the German government were simply manifestations of war-weariness and defeatism. In face of the coercive machinery of the state and the massive force of official propaganda, such protests were, of course, long ineffective; but three events gave them political weight. The first was the Russian revolution in March 1917, which gave new confidence to the workers in all countries, in particular in Germany. The second was the peace of Brest-Litovsk, imposed on Russia by the German High Command, which by opening the eyes of the German people to the unrepentant imperialism of their government, created a revolutionary atmosphere throughout the country. The third was President Wilson's enunciation, on January 7th, 1918, of the 'Fourteen Points', which — for those who were not aware that they constituted for England and France only (in the words of Wilson's confidant, Colonel House) 'an

admirable tool of propaganda' — appeared to offer a substantial basis
for a just peace. These events stimulated the German people to
proceed from protests and manifestos to action. In April 1917 a
great strike involving two hundred thousand workers took place
in Berlin and Leipzig, the main demands of the strikers being the
introduction of a democratic régime and immediate peace negotiations on the basis of 'no annexations'. More serious and more widespread were the munition workers' strikes in January 1918 — a
direct reply of the German people to the insolence and intransigence of the German negotiators at Brest-Litovsk — which occurred
at the very moment when Ludendorff was preparing his last gigantic
thrust against France, the famous spring offensive of 1918 designed
to secure a final German victory. The strikes were suppressed by
force; but they constituted none the less a clear manifestation of the
spirit of the German people, which at this critical period ignored the
appeals of the government to give all their strength for the last
decisive blow, and sought instead a peace of reconciliation on the
basis of the Fourteen Points. To the enduring credit of the German
people, the final overthrow of Hohenzollern imperialism was in no
small measure the result of the distrust and overt opposition maintained by German labour organizations.[1] The failure of Ludendorff's
spring offensive created the conditions for a renewal of the German
opposition, quelled in January 1918; and the German High Command, aware of the imminence of revolution, hastened to conclude
an armistice while the army was still intact. This decision was made
more urgent by the collapse of Bulgaria in September 1918 and the
crumbling of the Austrian front; complete military defeat, although
not yet a fact, was within sight and Ludendorff knew that a defensive
war — which, in the judgement of the French experts, was still
militarily possible — could not be fought in view of the revolutionary spirit in Germany. It was a typical decision that he determined
to make peace with the Entente before the army disintegrated, and
thus to conserve the armed forces as a political factor for use in
Germany. At the end of September the High Command abdicated

[1] Thus H. W. V. Temperley, *History of the Peace Conference*, I (1920), 213; cf. also General
Smuts' view (in his pamphlet, *The League of Nations*, 14): 'The German battlefront collapsed
the more readily before Foch because the scandalous Brest-Litovsk Treaty had thoroughly
disillusioned and demoralized the German people.' How enduring was the impression created
in Germany by Brest-Litovsk is indicated by Hitler's confession (recorded by Fraser, *Germany
between Two Wars*, 42) that his attempts, at a later date, to stir up popular resentment against
the Versailles Treaty were met by the cry: 'And Brest-Litovsk?'

the dictatorial powers which it had exercised since 1916 and a constitutional government was set up under prince Max of Baden with the avowed object of securing peace on the basis of the Fourteen Points; on November 11th, 1918 an armistice was concluded.

Only military defeat, neutralizing the armed power on which government rested, could destroy the rigid system of class domination and Prussian hegemony which Bismarck had fastened on the body of Germany in 1871. At no time between 1871 and 1918 was revolution within the bounds of practical politics; and internal revolution was the only alternative to military defeat as a means of getting rid of the system. Peaceful evolution under a parliamentary régime, which in England offered the people a constitutional means of making their aspirations heard and their interests felt, was excluded by the very character of the German constitution of 1871 which was designed, under the simulacrum of parliamentary government, to prevent peaceful evolution; this was evident — although many contemporary observers, particularly in England, failed to perceive it — in every crisis from 1894 to 1913. Undoubtedly the Bismarckian Reich, although eventually it rested on bare force, corresponded to and satisfied the interests of certain important groups in Germany; apart from the Junkers, to perpetuate whose power it was contrived, it furthered the interests of the powerful industrial and commercial classes, and could count at most times on the support of the important Catholic Centre party, which regarded it as a bulwark against social changes anathematized by the church. It was a rallying-point for all who had something to lose by popular government working for the interests of the people. More ominous for the future was the fact that an element in the labour and trades union movement, observing the indisputable improvement of wages and working conditions under the stimulus of capitalist expansion, was prepared to compromise with the existing system, in the belief that it could, by steady pressure, gradually be transformed into a political and social democracy. But such views, although they had some justification under English political conditions, were a delusion in imperialist Germany; and they were consistently rejected by the majority of Social Democrats. It was possible to maintain — as one of the minority wrote during the war years — that 'the ruin of German industry would be the ruin of the German working class'; but the working classes themselves, as they demonstrated in the political strikes which began in 1916, believed on the contrary that a victory for German imperialism and for German capitalism would be as crushing a defeat for them as for the workers in the enemy lands; it would rivet more firmly the privileges of the self-styled 'nationalist' classes and give a new lease of life to the constitution which in practice disfranchised the workers. Hence from 1917 onwards the anti-war movement grew. After the issue of the Fourteen Points defeat was not regarded with fear; for Wilson's declaration contained the promise of a saner international order, in which the German people, with the promise of democracy and self-determination, could take its place. The end of the war thus seemed to betoken the dawn of a new era under a republican government, expressing the will and promoting the interests of the German people; the defeat of Prussian militarism and of all that went with it seemed for the first time to offer the German people the opportunity of moulding its own destiny.

§ 21. *The Weimar Republic* (1919–1933)

The hopes and expectations roused in 1918 by the defeat of Hohenzollern militarism were doomed to disappointment; the opportunity to remodel German society and German political life in a new international framework was missed. Three main factors explain the failure. First, the army, the unswerving guardian of the old order, although defeated on the field of battle, remained in existence, a potent reactionary factor in German politics. Secondly, the German people was not left free to reshape German society on democratic lines; instead it was subjected to Allied pressure and, at many important points, to Allied veto, and the creation of an efficient government capable of expressing the will of the German people was subordinated to the national interests of the victorious Entente. Thirdly, the German leaders who emerged after the flight of William II on November 9th, 1918, proved totally incapable of rising to the magnitude of the tasks facing them; instead of placing themselves at the head of the revolutionary forces which the military failure had released, and carrying through a total reorganization of German society, they sought to steer a cautious middle course and let slip the opportunity for fundamental change which alone could have assured the prevalence of the strong democratic forces in Germany.

Nothing was clearer, after the experiences of the period 1871-1918, than the fact that without a real shift in economic and social power, transferring political initiative from the Junkers and capitalist interests to the people, the introduction of a lasting democratic régime was impossible. The revolution which began on November 3rd, 1918, with the naval mutiny at Kiel and spread rapidly through the whole country between November 6th and 9th, opened up the immediate prospect of fundamental change; for it was a spontaneous movement directed by workers' and soldiers' councils elected everywhere in workshops, mines, docks and barracks, and this movement, at its first congress in December 1918, formulated demands which included the socialization of key industries and, pending its replacement by a people's militia, a purge of the army. If put into effect, this programme would, without doubt, have brought about the fundamental shift in economic and political power which was the essential pre-condition for the success of the whole revolutionary movement. But it was not put into effect. Gröner, who had replaced Ludendorff on October 26th, as quartermaster-general, informed the government that he and the entire High Command would resign immediately, if the workers' proposals were put into effect; and before this ultimatum the government, although it was a Social Democratic government nominated by the workers' and soldiers' councils, capitulated. Instead of proceeding to the immediate socialization of industry at the moment when the workers' councils were in effective control of the workshops, it set up a 'Socialization Commission' with employers' and workers' representatives, which naturally failed to reach agreement and soon faded ineffectually out of existence. Instead of partitioning the great estates east of the Elbe, it appointed another commission to study the problem. Instead of convoking immediately a national assembly, it delayed elections until January 19th, 1919, and refused to take any decisive steps until the new assembly's authorization had been secured. Thus, through the anxious, cautious constitutionalism of the Social Democrat leaders, Ebert and Scheidemann, none of the three fundamental reforms — democratization of the army, public control of heavy industry, redistribution of landed property — was secured; and the reason was that to secure them it would have been necessary to rely on extra-parliamentary means and have recourse to popular pressure. Such a policy was alien to the whole character of the Social Democratic leadership, which had for decades past known no higher aim than the attainment of parliamentary democracy and the representation in parliament of working-class interests. No minister had the courage to accept the responsibility for using the power actually in his possession in order to change the internal balance of power or to secure control of its mainsprings. Hence the constituent assembly which met at Weimar to draft a new constitution in the spring of 1919 succeeded only in grafting mechanical devices, such as proportional representation, parliamentary sovereignty and the referendum, on to the existing body politic; but under this liberal cloak the old economic and political forces of the Hohenzollern empire continued to exist undisturbed. The Weimar Constitution established the external forms of political liberty, but without the changes in social and economic power which alone could give them vitality.

This initial failure, from which recovery in fact proved impossible, was not, of course, the result of a deliberate betrayal of the revolution by the Social Democrat leaders. It was due to the limitations of the men themselves, and it was due in part at least to external circumstances, before which they capitulated. They were afraid lest economic experiment might produce chaos, and expose Germany to the famine and misery from which Russia was then suffering. They were afraid lest social change, easily denounced as 'Bolshevism', might lead to Allied intervention. These fears were not unjustified. All the Entente powers were preoccupied with the dangers of 'Bolshevism' and particularly afraid of 'Bolshevik revolution' in Germany,[1] and were prepared to co-operate with the German army to preserve 'order' in Germany, just as they co-operated with it in the Baltic states and the Ukraine against the Russian revolution. Thus the German revolution was from the very beginning frustrated by the hostility of the victorious powers, and there is no reason to believe that they would have shrunk from the use of force and the

---

[1] 'Russia', said R. S. Baker, a member of the American delegation at the peace conference in Paris, 'played a more vital part at Paris than Prussia. Without ever being represented at Paris at all, the Bolsheviki and Bolshevism were powerful elements at every turn' (*Woodrow Wilson and World Settlement*, II, 64). How deep-seated fear of Bolshevism was, is revealed in a striking memorandum drawn up by Lloyd George, ibid. III, 449-457. 'As long as order was maintained in Germany', said Lloyd George, 'a breakwater would exist between the countries of the Allies and the waters of revolution beyond. But once that breakwater was swept away, he could not speak for France, and he trembled for his own country.'

terrible weapon of blockade, as occurred in the case of Hungary, had it proved necessary to oppose fundamental social change. In these circumstances a policy of radical social and economic reform undoubtedly entailed serious risks, and could not have been carried through without heavy sacrifices on the part of the German people, for which the rulers were unwilling to take responsibility. The failure of the Social Democrat leaders — and, indeed, of the Allied powers — was the failure to realize that these risks were no less serious than the dangers of doing nothing, which gave reaction the chance of recovery. Instead they concentrated their efforts, partly to keep Allied confidence, partly to prove their ability to govern, on the maintenance of law and order. Because they feared that their removal would have disturbed the smooth running of the public services, they left the officials of the old imperial bureaucracy in office; because they feared that his dismissal would complicate demobiliz-ation and worsen relations with the victorious Entente, they retained Hindenburg, and with him the core of the old army. Worse still, the preoccupation of the government with law and order brought it into conflict with the very forces whose spontaneous action had brought about the November revolution of 1918. This conflict came to a head in January 1919, when the Social Democrat defence minister, Gustav Noske, called in the notorious Free Corps to crush the left-wing labour movement in Berlin, and followed up this success by a series of punitive expeditions extending from Bremen to Munich. The civil war which raged for the first three months of 1919 sealed the fate of the German republic; the victory of Ebert and Noske was hailed as a victory for the middle-class republic and democracy over Bolshevism, but in reality it was a victory for the Free Corps, for the anti-democratic forces which had come to the rescue of the republic to prevent social change, but which only tolerated the republican government temporarily as the lesser evil. On the other hand, it created a breach between the right and left wings of the German labour movement so deep that it could never again be bridged; and this breach permanently crippled the powers of resistance of the democratic forces when reaction had sufficiently recovered to raise its head. The attitude of the people to the repub-lican government was aptly described as early as June 1919, by one of the more foresighted Social Democrat ministers, Rudolf Wissell; 'in spite of the Revolution', he said:—

the hopes of the people have been disappointed. The government
has not lived up to the expectations of the people. We have, indeed,
constructed a formal political democracy, but fundamentally we
have done no more than continue the programme initiated by the
imperial government of Prince Max of Baden. We drew up the
constitution without real participation by the people. We failed to
satisfy the masses, because we had no proper programme.

Essentially, we have governed in the old ways, and there has been
little sign of a new spirit informing the old procedure. We have not
been able to influence the course of the Revolution in such a way that
Germany is swayed by a new inspiration. The essential character of
German civilization and social life is little altered, and that little not
always for the better. The people believes that the achievements of
the Revolution are of a merely negative character, that the only
change is in the set of persons exercising military and bureaucratic
authority, and that the present principles of government do not differ
in essentials from those of the old régime . . . It is my belief that the
verdict of history on the national assembly and on us, the members of
the government, will be hard and bitter.[1]

The attitude of profound disillusion with the Republic reflected in
Wissell's speech of June 14th, 1919, was confirmed by the terms of the
peace settlement, which was signed a few days later, on June 28th.
It is no part of our business to enter into the unending controversy
which, ever since 1919, has centred round the Treaty of Versailles,
its relation to Wilson's Fourteen Points and to the fundamental
principle of 'self-determination' on which they were based.[2] It is
enough to note that certain facts impressed themselves on Germans
of all parties. First, the settlement was 'dictated', i.e. contrary to previous international practice the French representative, Clemenceau,
prevented verbal negotiations. Secondly, in spite of Allied lip-
service to the principles of 'self-determination' wide areas were
detached from Germany without plebiscite,[3] the *Anschluss* of
Germany and Austria was vetoed by France, and over three and a

---

[1] A. Rosenberg, *Gesch. d. deutschen Republik* (1935), 105.

[2] There is a careful summary, free from propagandist bias, by Henderson, 'The Peace Settlement, 1919', in *History*, XXVI (1941), 60–69; the historian will be well advised to consult this
survey, and the literature there referred to, and to avoid unreliable propaganda published
more recently.

[3] Cf. Henderson, op. cit., 65–66: 'In the east Germany lost nine-tenths of Posen and two-
thirds of West Prussia without a plebiscite.' In 'Upper Silesia', which 'had been under German
rule in one form or another for six centuries', although 'nearly sixty per cent of those who
went to the polls voted for Germany', 'the new frontier gave the Poles five-sixths of the industrial area and eighty per cent of the coal-bearing region'.

half million Germans, who actively sought incorporation in the new Austrian republic, were compelled by Czech troops led by French officers to remain in the new Czechoslovak state. Thirdly, despite the assurance of a 'free, open-minded and absolutely impartial adjustment of all colonial claims', Germany was deprived of all her colonies without a formal hearing. Fourthly, the German representatives were compelled — in contradiction to Wilson's promise of December 4th, 1917, that 'no people shall be ... punished because the responsible rulers of a single country have themselves done deep and abominable wrong' — to sign a statement that Germany, along with the other defeated powers, 'accepted the responsibility' for causing all the loss and damage brought about by a war 'imposed upon' the world 'by the aggression of Germany and her allies'. Fifthly, on the basis of this clause 'reparations' amounting to 132 milliard gold marks were demanded, i.e. twenty-two times the amount demanded of Russia by the German imperial government in the notorious treaty of Brest-Litovsk.[1] Juridically, it is possible to justify most, if not all, of these terms as part of a settlement imposed by a conqueror on a vanquished enemy; but they were a serious blow to the forces of German democracy which, confident in the promises of Wilson and Lloyd George,[2] sincerely believed that Germany, once it had overthrown the Hohenzollerns and broken, under a democratic régime, with the traditions of Hohenzollern imperialism, could count on terms such as would enable the republic to take its place in the comity of nations. Instead it was saddled with 'guilt' for the policy of William II, in which it had no share and which it had rejected. The inexpediency of this policy, the moving spirit behind which was France, was recognized at the time by both Wilson and Lloyd George;[3] but, with their hands tied by secret treaties con-

[1] This is described by Fraser, *Germany between Two Wars* (1941), 61, as 'a big advance in leniency towards the defeated side'.

[2] For example, Lloyd George's speech of January 5th, 1918, to a congress of Trade Union delegates, summed up in a Labour party manifesto in the following terms: 'it reveals a government and a people seeking no selfish and predatory aims of any kind, pursuing with one mind one unchanging purpose: to obtain justice for others so that we thereby secure for ourselves a lasting peace. We desire neither to destroy Germany nor diminish her boundaries; we seek neither to exalt ourselves nor to enlarge our Empire'.

[3] In the memorandum referred to above p. 140, n. 1, for example, Lloyd George wrote: 'You may strip Germany of her colonies, reduce her armaments to a mere police force and her navy to that of a fifth-rate power; all the same in the end if she feels that she has been unjustly treated in the peace of 1919 she will find means of exacting retribution from her conquerors ... I would, therefore, put it in the forefront of the peace that ... we will ... do everything possible to enable the German people to get upon their legs again.'

cluded during the war, neither was able to put up a firm opposition to the policy of Clemenceau, and once again, as so often in the past, the possibility of lasting European peace was sacrificed to the national interests of France. French demands for the annexation of the Saar and the separation of the Rhineland from Germany were successfully resisted; but French policy created ineradicable suspicions and there were few Germans — or, for the matter of that, few Americans or Englishmen — who did not believe that the principle of national 'self-determination', as applied in the case of Poland and Czechoslovakia, had been used as a cloak for a French attempt to raise clients in the east, whose political function was to aid France in perpetuating Germany's defeat. Such a view was unjust to Wilson and Lloyd George; but it faithfully reflected the spirit of Clemenceau's policy.[1] By pursuing the inflexible aims of unrepentant power politics at the moment when in Germany — and, indeed, in England and America and throughout Europe — a new generation, reacting against pre-war imperialism, was prepared to renounce power-politics as an instrument of national interests, France destroyed the hopes of 1919.[2] In Germany, the effects of this policy were disastrous. By treating the new German republic as a weak and defeated power, French policy equated the republic and weakness and thereby strengthened immeasurably the hand of all reactionary forces within Germany opposed to the republic. 'The outcome', as a leading English historian has said, 'has been the Germany of Hitler that we know.'[3]

[1] When Clemenceau's failure to secure Anglo-American adhesion to his plans for the disintegration of Germany led to a major political crisis in the French cabinet on April 25th, 1919, he won his point by a speech addressed to Poincaré, in which he said: 'Mr. President, you are much younger than I am. In fifteen years I shall no longer be alive. In fifteen years the Germans will not have fulfilled the conditions of the treaty. If you will then do me the honour of visiting my grave, I am convinced you will be able to tell me: We are on the Rhine, and there we remain!' Still more open was Poincaré's own remark in 1922: 'We are simply — and I feel very well in so doing — going towards the permanent occupation of the left bank of Rhine' (cf. Haller, France and Germany, 271-272).

[2] In the words of Lloyd George, 'the dead hand of Poincaré lay heavy on Europe'; cf. G. P. Gooch, 'British Foreign Policy, 1919-38,' Studies in Diplomacy and Statecraft (1942), 175.

[3] Cf. G. M. Trevelyan, British History in the Nineteenth Century and After (1937), 483-85: 'The great error of the Treaty was the harsh treatment of the new German Republic. It should have been the first object of England and France to enable it to survive as a peaceful democracy. But the German nation was humiliated by the dictation of terms on the hardships of which she was not even permitted to plead before the victors; she was kept disarmed while other nations (though not England) remained armed to the teeth; she was forbidden to unite with Austria; she was excluded from the League of Nations; in the matter of reparations she was treated in a manner so fantastic as to help to ruin her without benefiting her creditors . . . France could not change or forget. She not only refused to disarm, but continued for years to harass the

To follow in detail the well-known story of the years from 1919 to 1933, from Versailles to Hitler, is not necessary, for in all essentials, due to the folly of the Allies and the failures of the German democratic leaders, the die was, as early as 1919, already cast. From the start, the Weimar republic failed to arouse the enthusiasm or anchor the loyalties of the great majority of Germans. On the right, the nationalist sections, which still wielded immense pressure, regarded it as a transitory stage on the road towards the reassertion both of their old preponderance at home and of German military power in Europe. On the left, the bulk of the German people regarded it as an equally transitory stage towards a form of political organization which really reflected popular aspirations. What backing it had came from the middle classes; but owing to the unbalanced development of German society from the time of the Thirty Years War onwards, the middle classes were too weak and politically too unreliable to carry alone the burden of government, and if they had to choose between the left, with the threat of real social change, and the reactionary groups of the right, they preferred co-operation with the latter. This weakness played into the hands of the right-wing sections, which soon established themselves in a position of control, enabling them to use the constitutional machinery of government for their own ends. It played into the hands of the Reichswehr which, in 1923, forced the working-class governments of Saxony and Thuringia to resign. Still more ominous, it played into the hands of the industrialists, who after November 1922 loosed the horrors of inflation on Germany in order, while freeing themselves from internal indebtedness, to destroy the resources of organized labour. With the appointment of Wilhelm Cuno, a director of the Hamburg-Amerika line, as prime minister in 1923, the undisguised rule of large-scale capital began;[1] the attack on the Eight Hour Day and the refusal to meet expenditure by direct taxation revealed that the notorious Hugo Stinnes and Fritz Thyssen were in the saddle. Heavy industry prospered as never before, while the nation was starving and the state facing bankruptcy; from 1920 to 1924 the

German Republic, thus preparing the way for its transformation into the Nazi régime . . . The outcome has been the Germany of Hitler that we know.' — Gooch (*Studies in Diplomacy and Statecraft*, 163), summing up the results of Versailles, says: 'Its unexpected severity struck the frail Weimar Republic a blow from which it never recovered, for democracy was identified in many German minds with humiliation and defeat.'

[1] Rosenberg, op. cit., 95. Fraser, op. cit., 88, describes the economic policy of the Cuno government as 'an integral part of the great conspiracy against the German people'.

power of capital increased immensely, and its hold was consolidated after 1924 in the course of reconstruction and rationalization and the progress of industrial monopoly.[1]

These tendencies were concealed but in no way reversed by the period of relative prosperity between 1924 and 1929. The fact that business, supported by foreign loans, was again back to normal brought a gradual slackening of tension, particularly in the industrial field, and it seemed as though democracy was at last functioning properly and booking results in the form of improved housing conditions and similar social benefits. But the effect of such social services, however welcome in themselves, on German economic structure was nil, and under the surface the old balance of power persisted. The election of Hindenburg to the presidency in 1925 was an index of the true situation; it revealed in a flash how far removed from power the democratic and progressive forces were in the midtwenties. Although 'the great majority of Germans' wanted to 'settle down to a life of peace and international co-operation',[2] the power of heavy industry, which ultimately could only keep going on the basis of a great armaments programme, continued to expand. The desire of the German people for a continuation of peace and democratic government was expressed in the elections of 1928, when the Social Democratic vote, which had slumped in 1921 and 1923, rose to over nine millions, and the two working-class parties, the Social Democrats and the Communists, together secured over 42 per cent of the seats in the Reichstag. But this swing in the voting, unaccompanied by any move to break the economic and social power of the industrial and landed classes, did not imply a fundamental strengthening of democratic government. It only needed a break in prosperity to bring back into the open the antagonism between the army and the great industrial monopolies on the one hand,

[1] The two most powerful German trusts were formed during this period, the I. G. Farbenindustrie (i.e. the German Dye Trust) in 1925, and the Vereinigte Stahlwerke (United Steel Works) in 1926.

[2] Thus Lindsay, *Germany between Two Wars*, 77-78. Elsewhere he concedes that there is 'every reason to believe that the war aspirations of the men behind the scenes were not shared by the German people. In 1926 a member of the Reichstag, Philipp Scheidemann, had discovered the arrangements in force for building aeroplanes and training crews in Russia. This revelation caused an immense sensation in Germany, and the reaction of the ordinary German was thoroughly hostile. Two years later, when the question of building a new battle-cruiser came up before the Reichstag, the proposal, though entirely in conformity with the Treaty of Versailles, was violently opposed by the left-wing parties and was only in the 'end forced through with the utmost difficulty'. But 'the constitutional government of Germany was not strong enough to enforce a policy of peace upon the fanatics behind the scenes' (ibid., 84).

and the people on the other. This came in 1929. Already by February 1929 the total number of unemployed had passed the three million mark. In October 1929 there followed the Wall Street crash. Short-term loans — fifty per cent of the loans to Germany totalling twenty milliard marks were short-term, unconsolidated loans—were recalled; German industry, dependent on foreign markets because low wages and drastic inequalities of income prevented the creation of a great domestic market, slumped rapidly; and unemployment increased apace. By January 1933 official unemployment figures passed the six million mark, but the actual number of unemployed rose to between eight and nine millions.

§ 22. *National Socialism and the German People* (1933-1939)

The crisis which set in during 1929 brought about the death of the German republic. Having failed to enlist the support of the working classes, the republic was dependent upon the middle-class vote of the centre parties. But the middle classes, the small property owners and shopkeepers, who had already been hit by·the inflation, collapsed before the slump of 1929-1933; the rapid decline in the workers' purchasing power ruined millions of small shopkeepers, tradesmen, artisans, black-coated workers and peasants, and these elements — which had, as a class, nothing to hope from a working-class movement — turned to Hitler and the specious promises of National Socialism. The National Socialist vote, which had rallied only 800,000 supporters in 1923, rose in September ·1930 to almost 6,500,000, and the National Socialists emerged from insignificance to the position of second strongest party in the Reichstag. Two years later, in July 1932, the vote for Hitler more than doubled, rising to 13,700,000 out of a total electorate of some 45,000,000 — the highest vote ever obtained by National Socialism in a free election. This success, born of the crisis, was secured at the expense of the middle- and upper-class parties; as indicated in the table below,[1] the working-class electorate — in spite of the miseries of poverty and unemployment — tenaciously resisted the blandishments of Hitler's demagogy, and the working-class vote, cast in favour of

---

[1] Quoted from E. Anderson, *Hammer or Anvil. The Story of the German working-class movement* (1945), 141, whose careful analyses may be consulted for further detail.

Social Democracy and Communism, stood firm throughout, just as the Catholic vote stood firm. The split in the left-wing forces, and in particular the purblind policy of the Communist leaders, unhappily facilitated the rise of National Socialism; but the real strength of Hitlerism lay in the support of the privileged classes,

VOTES (IN MILLIONS) AT GENERAL ELECTIONS, 1924-1932

Parties	1924	1928	1930	July 1932	Nov. 1932
Working-class parties (Social Democrats and Communists)	10.5	12.3	13.0	13.1	13.1
Middle-class parties (excluding Centre party)	13.2	12.9	10.3	4.0	5.3
Catholic Centre Party	4.1	3.7	4.1	4.5	4.2
National Socialists	0.9	0.8	6.4	13.7	11.7

of the industrial 'kings', the Junkers and the army, with the connivance of parallel interests in England and France. At no stage from the onset of the crisis in 1929 until 1933 had Hitler any hope of succeeding to power, even by unconstitutional means, without the backing of capitalist and reactionary interests. Before the inauguration of the Hitler terror National Socialism never obtained the support of more than one-third of the German people; and in the last six months of 1932 National Socialist strength actually decreased by 2,000,000 votes. When on January 30th, 1933 Hitler was made chancellor, it was not through the support of, but rather as the result of a conspiracy against the German people: his rise to power was the work of Hindenburg representing the army, of Papen representing the aristocracy, of Hugenberg, the press-lord, and of Thyssen representing the industrialists of the Ruhr. It was this unholy alliance which led the German people to ruin and Europe to war.

The alliance with National Socialism, contrived by Hugenberg as early as 1929 and formally concluded by Papen at the beginning of 1933, was only the last step in a campaign against the democratic republic and the German people waged by the 'national' interests ever since the onset of the economic crisis in 1929. For these interests the depression was a welcome opportunity — 'this', one industrialist declared, 'is the crisis we need!' — to break for ever the power of the German people to guide their own destinies, and in particular to destroy organized labour. As in the inflation they had attacked the Eight Hour Day, so in 1930 they immediately launched an attack on the unemployment fund, while resisting the Social Democratic attempt to impose direct taxes. The resignation of the Social Democrat ministers and the appointment of Brüning as chancellor in March 1930 marked their success, and the end of democratic government in Germany. Thenceforward government was in the hands of a narrow clique, which, supported by the army and the executive under Hindenburg, dispensed with constitutional forms and ruled by emergency decrees. These decrees were directed ruthlessly against the working classes: indirect taxation was increased, new capitation taxes were introduced, bearing as heavily on the poor as on the rich, food prices were forced up in the interests of the agriculturists by heavy import duties. At the same time a devastating policy of deflation was introduced to support German export industries, and huge sums were paid out as subsidies to the bankrupt Junker agriculturists east of the Elbe. It was class rule on a huge scale, unashamedly pursuing class interests at the expense of the people; its naked use of force was seen when on July 20th, 1932, Papen ousted the constitutional labour government of Prussia and entrusted executive power to General von Rundstedt. But it was class rule on a narrow foundation. The working-class parties, as has been seen, remained firm, holding the allegiance of their traditional supporters to the last; but the 'nationalist' parties underwent a disastrous decline. The scandals of the *Osthilfe*, the endless government subsidies to its Junker supporters, could not be hushed up; the demand for a re- distribution of the land in eastern Germany for the benefit of the people could not be quelled. On the other hand, there were limits, even in Germany in 1933, to an unconcealed dictatorship based on the armed forces. For landowners and industrialists alike the sharp decline in the National Socialist vote in November 1932 and the signs of a swing to the extreme left, were ominous trends, alarming indications that the day of reckoning was at hand. Their alliance with Hitler was the sequel. It was an alliance reluctantly entered into; but, their own supporters having disintegrated, it was necessary as a device to throw a cloak of popular support over the dictatorship which, under a rotting veil, they had exercised ever since the Social Democrats were forced out of office in March 1930.

The calculations of the 'national' industrial and Junker interests miscarried. When on January 30th, 1933, Hindenburg and Papen called in Hitler, hoping thereby to stabilize their own hold over Germany, they gave themselves and Germany a new master, implacable and ruthless. They thought they had secured an instrument for the enslavement of the German people; but although Hitler ruthlessly destroyed German labour, he was no instrument of the reactionaries and the industrial capitalists. Through a deliberate policy of brute repression and armed might he manœuvred the National Socialist party — still a minority party, supported by less than 44 per cent of the electorate, even after the burning of the Reichstag and the proscription and persecution of the Communists[1] — into a position of unassailable preponderance; but his dominion was not based on brute force alone. The régime of regimentation, the extirpation of working-class leaders, the abolition of rights of assembly and discussion and the suppression of freedom of speech and of the press, played their part, preventing any organization of the workers as a political and social force and leaving the individual helpless in face of the machinery of party and state; but at the same time Hitler took positive steps to win majority support for National Socialism. He promised more than any other party offered; and for a time, from 1933 to 1938, he seemed to keep his promises. He promised work, and in fact he conquered unemployment, though only through a vast rearmament programme. He promised peace — 'National Socialist Germany', he said in 1935, 'desires peace from its deepest inner creed and conviction' — and at the same time a righting

---

[1] At the elections held on March 5th, 1933, in spite of intimidation and terror, the National Socialists won only 288 seats out of 647, as compared with 120 for the Social Democrats, 81 for the Communists, 73 for the Catholic Centre, and 52 for the German Nationalists. The Social Democrats lost only one seat, the Communists (already declared illegal and rounded up into concentration camps) only nineteen; the Catholic Centre even won three new seats. It was only through the adhesion of the right-wing Nationalists and by declaring the Communist vote illegal, that the National Socialists, even after five weeks of repression, could claim an absolute majority.

of the injustices done at Versailles; and in annulling the demilitariz-
ation of the Rhineland in 1936, and in securing the *Anschluss* with
Austria in 1938 and the incorporation, six months later, of the
Sudeten Germans into the Reich without war, he seemed to have
kept his promise. His success was the more impressive because, as
late as 1931, French opposition had prevented the union of Germany
and Austria, thereby driving another French nail into the coffin of
the German republic; after 1936 many in Germany who had spon-
sored peaceful negotiation were forced to admit that in a world
dominated by power politics armed force had achieved incisive
results beyond the capacity of the peaceful policy of the Republic.
Yet, in fact, Hitler's successes in foreign policy were due less to
German rearmament, the deficiencies and limitations of which
were known in competent military circles, than to the tacit alliance
of powerful reactionary elements in England and France, which,
though loath to see a reassertion of German equality, were still more
unwilling to check it by military alliance with Soviet Russia or to
run the risk of social revolution as a result of Hitler's fall. Just as, at
home, Hitler commended himself to the right-wing 'nationalist'
parties by his attack on labour, so abroad he was hailed as the saviour
of Europe from Communism; when, in 1938, his policy seemed to be
leading directly to war with Czechoslovakia, which in the opinion
of the High Command would have been 'catastrophic' for Germany,
it was the intervention of the English premier, Chamberlain, which
saved him from deposition by the German army.[1] But if Hitler
secured the support of German and European reaction, he did not
make the mistake of identifying himself with the reactionary cause.
His party was, in theory, a 'socialist' party, and had in its early days
undoubtedly incorporated genuine socialist elements; and even
after the 'blood bath' of June 30th, 1934, when the section in the
party which hoped for social revolution was eliminated, National
Socialist propaganda took care to pay court to what Hitler described
as 'the anti-capitalist longing of the masses'. In fact, none of the

---

[1] The facts about the army plot to get rid of Hitler, timed to take effect on September 14th–
15th, 1938, are well attested. The references published in the *Times* of March 15th, 1946,
are garbled and inaccurate; but a full and reliable summary of the official report appeared
in the *Daily Worker* of September 12th, 1945. According to the official report, 'public
opinion in Germany was very favourable . . . as the idea of war filled everyone with
horror'. But the intervention of Chamberlain on September 14th changed everything.
'The prospect of war receded' and (in the words of the *Times*) Hitler 'could pose before
the German people as the peacemaker'.

'socialist' demands which figured in the official National Socialist programme was ever put into effect; but the importance of Hitler's 'social demagogy' should not for that reason be underrated.[1] Above all else it gave foundation to his claim to stand for the interests of the whole German people, and thus differentiated his policy from that of the old 'nationalist' parties, whose pursuit of class-interests was barefaced. Even in this last phase, therefore, the long-standing conflict between the interests and aims of the ruling classes and the interests of the German people, deftly exploited by Nazi propaganda, played its part. The long-felt desire for a Germany of the German people, the hope which had arisen and been dashed in 1848 and again in 1918, was taken up and exploited by the leaders of the revolution of 1933. Hitler — claiming, like Napoleon, to represent better than any assembly the will of the people — denounced democratic and parliamentary government as merely a cloak for the pursuit of sectional interests at the expense of the people; and of parliamentary government as it functioned in Germany between 1918 and 1933 this denunciation was not untrue. The insistence of National Socialist philosophy and propaganda on the 'folk' was not, as is often assumed, designed simply as part of a theory of racial superiority; its essential purpose at home was to emphasize the popular foundations of National Socialist rule, and writers of the period between 1933 and 1939 never tired of praising the National Socialist achievement in identifying 'folk' and 'state'. After generations in which the German people had been held at arm's length and divorced from politics, Hitler claimed to have consummated the unity of state and folk, of government and governed.

The claim was false. In the present state of knowledge we do not know, and — due to deliberate Nazi falsification — we probably never shall know, how implicitly the German people accepted Hitler's professions; but it is certain that any trust placed by Germany in Hitler was betrayed. He worked for war, although (as he rightly said) 'if leaders and rulers only desire peace, the people have never

---

[1] The 'Twenty-Five Points' of 1920, in which the programme of the National Socialist party was enunciated, are printed in Oakeshott, *The Social and Political Doctrines of Contemporary Europe* (1939), 190 sqq. They include abolition of unearned income and 'emancipation from the slavery of interest charges' (§.11), confiscation of war profits (§.12), nationalization of trusts (§.13), introduction of profit sharing (§.14), 'communalization' of the big departmental stores (§.16), a programme of agrarian reform including 'confiscation without compensation' of land for communal purposes (§.17); cf. also §§.15, 18 (death penalty for usury and profiteering), 20, 21.

wanted war'. He promised the destruction of 'interest slavery' and liberation from 'monopoly capitalism'; but he destroyed the defences built up by the German working classes against the evils of German industrialism and betrayed the German people into the hands of the very industrial and agrarian interests from which he claimed to have rescued them. His government was based not, as he represented, on popular mandate, but on an alliance with financial and military interests which differed only from earlier alliances in so far as the National Socialist party and not the interests concerned retained the upper hand. He feared the people, as much as the forces of German reaction feared the people, and therefore he stifled every free expression of popular will, because, like the 'national' interests, he recognized the deep cleft between his own objectives and the aspirations of the German people. When National Socialist policy unleashed war on September 1st, 1939, the attitude of the German people was, in the words of a competent American observer, 'the most striking demonstration against war I have ever seen';[1] but an expression of the views and will of the German people was even more impossible in 1939 than it had been under Hohenzollern imperialism. For Hitler the German people was, as he said, 'a flock of sheep', fit only for obedience, which had to be dragooned into the 'nationalist' path. From 1933 to 1939 he pursued this dragooning with a skill which it would be a fatal error to underestimate and with effects the durability of which time alone can prove or disprove; by repressing opposition, by perverting education, by exploiting genuine grievances and by conferring limited benefits, he fastened on Germany a régime hostile to all the German people had striven after, ever since, between 1815 and 1848, that same people first asserted the right to control its own destinies. This fundamental right, denied for long centuries before 1848, was never securely grasped at any stage between 1815 and 1939; the opposing interests consecrated by history, were too strongly entrenched. But the problem still remains, the enduring legacy of German history, to build a Germany of the German people, representing not the will of a predatory minority, but the sober interests and aspirations of the German-speaking millions in the historic German lands between France and the Slavonic east.

[1] W. L. Shirer, *Berlin Diary* (1941), 119. This and other eye-witness reports are collected by Anderson, op. cit., 183.

RETROSPECT

IT is no part of the object of the present volume to outline an approach to the problem of Germany which confronts the world to-day. But few readers, looking back retrospectively over the preceding pages, will easily escape certain reflections or fail to be struck by certain well-defined lines of development which are implicit in the course of German history. The problem of modern Germany cannot be discussed without consideration of economic and geo-political factors and of contemporary political doctrines and divisions which have no place in a work such as this. But it is essential that the historical and human background against which such factors play out their rôle should be widely understood and accurately interpreted; for it is beyond doubt that a living consciousness of the past plays a formative part in current problems, influencing men's reactions to the stark economic facts and political dilemmas with which they have to cope. The German reaction, beginning in the days of Bismarck, to the crisis of modern industrial capitalism is only comprehensible in the light of Germany's past; political and social conditions inherited from remote generations determined the specific character of that reaction and explain the salient differences in the simultaneous approach to similar problems in Germany and in France or England. Factors deeply rooted in German history — both in the history of the German people in relation to their governments and in the history of the German states in relation to the other states of Europe — constituted an iron framework or mould, within which all German efforts, from 1870 to 1939, to cope with the problems of modern capitalist society were cast. Anyone attempting to visualize the German problem of to-day and to find clues to a lasting settlement must, therefore, take heed of the past as it lives on in human consciousness as an integral part of the present; for the living past is the hard core of the German problem.

The value of the historical approach is that it enables us to set contemporary events and current problems against the background of the past and to see them in perspective; it is a safeguard against distortion and against hasty reaction. The temptation to analyse the German problem of to-day in the light of the present and of the immediate past is great; but there can be no valid assessment which does not cast wider and place in firm perspective the familiar events of the nineteenth and twentieth centuries. The German problem is not simply the problem of National Socialism — although, as we have seen, the National Socialist leaders took care to enlist support by promising to remedy the unsolved problems which were the legacy of German history — and its roots reach back far beyond Hitler's seizure of power in 1933, the Versailles settlement of 1919, or the Franco-Prussian War of 1870. Disentangled from inessentials it is the problem of a nation whose historical development has been retarded or arrested at a number of fundamental points. German history is a story of discontinuity, of development cut short, of incompleteness and retardation. The consolidation of the early monarchy was cut short in 1076; the work of Frederick Barbarossa was undermined by the papacy between 1198 and 1215; the establishment of national unity was fatally checked after 1250; the growth of representative institutions withered after the Reformation; the expansion of the middle classes was halted as a result of the Thirty Years War; the Peace of Westphalia subjected German political life for a century and a half to the dictates of French policy; the settlement of 1815 prolonged particularism; the growth of self-government was stunted by the constitution of 1871; the transfer of social and economic power was sidetracked in 1918 and 1919. These are the dates and facts which stand out as we survey in retrospect the long course of German development; and it is against this background that the most recent phases of German history must be reviewed. These dates and events are significant because they are the occasions on which the deep, underlying currents in German history come to the surface. Two factors, interlocked and inseparable, run like red threads through German history and together constitute the substantial legacy of Germany's past to Germany's present. The one is the demand for national unity, the other the quest for political institutions guaranteeing self-government; and it is the struggle to realize these two deep-lying aspirations, in spite of all obstacles, that gives sense and coherence to German history.

First in point of time was the struggle for German unity. No feature of German history is more remarkable than the persistence through the centuries of a sense of unity, reaching back in unbroken continuity to the tenth century. 'The typical German', it has been well said, 'turned in disgust and despair from a political reality eternally uncompleted and inadequate',[1] and never surrendered the hope of restoring the unity shattered between 1250 and 1356. The demand for *Reichsreform*, for national cohesion and a national policy, began in the fifteenth century;[2] but it involved a ceaseless struggle against enemies both at home and abroad, against princely particularism and against French encroachments and French interference in German affairs. The struggle against particularism lasted until 1871, and was doubtfully won even then; for, as we have seen, the solution of 1871 was really the triumph of the most successful of German particularisms.[3] The struggle against French encroachments, which began as early as the thirteenth century, was even longer and more bitter. French interference in German affairs, already long endemic, was reduced in 1648 into a European system designed to perpetuate German division and impotence for the benefit of France. The principles enshrined in the Peace of Westphalia were solemnly reaffirmed by the Directory and remained the basis of French policy, after the revolution of 1789, down to 1871; and even after 1871 German unity was never secure against the machinations of France which — adopting the battle-cry of 'revenge' — refused to accept the restitution to Germany of the conquests of Louis XIV and Louis XV and never finally renounced the age-old ambitions of the Rhine frontier, bridgeheads across the Rhine, the Saar valley and the dismemberment of Germany.

One root of the German problem of to-day is undeniably to be found in inveterate French resistance, on the pretext of 'security', to legitimate German aspirations for national unity, in the desire until 1870 to perpetuate and in 1918 and 1945 to renew German divisions, and so to pin Germany down permanently in a position of inferiority. Other strong roots lead back, through the generations, from 1648 to the far-off days at the end of the eleventh century when the old German monarchy, in the person of Henry IV, suffered defeat at the hands of German particularism in alliance with the papacy. In the middle ages the only effective guardian of the common heritage was a powerful monarchy, capable of suppressing sectional

---

[1] E. Vermeil, *Germany's Three Reichs* (1944), p. 45.
[2] Cf. above, p. 61 sqq.   [3] Cf. above, p. 121.

interests; and the lasting result of the events of 1076-1106 was that Germany, unlike England and France, forewent the benefits of effective monarchical government and after 1250 fell under the dominion of a princely aristocracy which, powerfully aided by foreign intervention, strengthened its hold in the centuries that followed. Princely particularism, the unlimited sovereignty of the princes, was, as Bismarck said, 'a revolutionary acquisition won at the expense of the nation'. By stifling the development of the middle classes and accumulating social and economic privileges in the hands of the few, it prevented the peaceful evolution of German political life into democratic forms capable of expressing the will of the German people. In spite of the growing demand after 1815 and still more after the rise of organized labour in the days of Bismarck for popular self-government in accordance with popular interests, progress towards representative institutions was blocked until 1918; and even after 1918 such institutions were never safe against the machinations of the privileged minority possessing social and economic power. Through Bismarck's tactical skill, through the caution and timidity of the leaders of 1918, and finally through the alliance of reaction and privilege with Hitlerism, the popular forces suffered defeat.

Historical analysis thus reveals, as the enduring legacy of German history, the two unsolved problems of unity and democracy; and we cannot expunge this legacy by ignoring its existence. If, on the other hand, the aspirations of the German people to unity and self-government are treated merely as off-shoots of National Socialism, there is a serious risk of fostering the survival of the National Socialist spirit in Germany, in exactly the same way as in 1919 failure to distinguish between Hohenzollern imperialism and the will of the German people expressed in the Republic helped to rekindle the spirit of German nationalism. National Socialism, discredited and overthrown, can be transformed into a danger even at this stage if, through the failure of European statesmen to satisfy the deep aspirations of the German people, it is again allowed to identify itself with the two great currents of German history. What is necessary is rather the elimination of the factors which, through the ages, have retarded German development, in order to prepare the way for Germany, purged of National Socialism, to take its place as an equal partner in Europe; and the way to achieve this lies in completing, not in thwarting, German aspirations to unity and popular self-government, in carrying through in a framework of German unity the process of democratization checked in 1918 and 1919. Democracy, as the history of the Weimar Republic served to show, cannot prosper in Germany without national unity and without equality for the German people in its dealings with other nations; and unity without democracy, as was proved between 1871 and 1918, is no guarantee of European peace. If Germany is to cease to be a danger-spot in Europe, it can only be through the creation of a united, democratic Germany within its historic boundaries; the forces at play are too deep-rooted and too vital for any other solution to endure. Such a solution, marching with history and renouncing the vain attempt to reverse history's march, is imperative because the German problem has never, in the whole course of German history, been a separate problem which can be isolated from the other problems of Europe. The unity of Europe depends on the unity of Germany, and what is at stake is not the fate of Germany alone but the fate of Europe. Without a settlement of the German question which, removing the age-old bars to German unity and German democracy, permits the German people to take its place as an equal partner in the comity of European nations, there can be no lasting settlement in Europe. That is why it is essential to survey objectively the determinative factors in German history and to apply unflinchingly the knowledge which only understanding of the living past can give.

INDEX

INDEX

Aachen, 23
Abodrites, 42
Adalbert, archbishop of Prague, 53
Adolf of Nassau (1292-1298), 29, 30
Africa, scramble for colonies in, 127-8
Albrecht I (1298-1308), 29, 45
Albrecht II (1438-1439), 52, 55, 56
Albrecht Achilles of Brandenburg (1471-1486), 49
Albrecht 'the Bear' of Brandenburg (1134-1170), 45
Albrecht the Wise of Upper Bavaria (1467-1508), 49
Alemannia, *see* Swabia
Alfonso of Castile, 27
Alsace, 29, 40, 57, 58, 70, 79, 83, 84
Anhalt, 21
Ansbach, 100
Arles, kingdom of, 39
Arnulf of Carinthia (887-899), 7, 9
Augsburg, 74; Peace of (1555), 64, 68, 75; Diet of (1530), 68
Austria, 19, 29, 36, 46-7, 55, 59, 75, 78-84; duke of, 31; and Prussia, in 18th century, 99-101, in 19th century, 111 *sqq.*; *Anschluss* with Germany, 151
Avignon, 30, 39

Bach, J. S., 85
Baden, 102, 104, 113, 123; Treaty of (1714), 80
Balkan Wars, 132
Baltic Sea, 40, 42
Bamberg, 24
Bar, 39, 83
Basel, 58; Treaty of (1795), 101
Bavaria, 9-10, 19, 21, 47, 69, 75, 77-8, 80, 91 *n*, 102, 107, 121, 123; duchy of, 4-5, 7; elector of, 83
Bayreuth, 100
Benedict XII (1334-1342), 30
Benno, Bishop of Osnabrück, 11
Berg, grand duchy of, 106
Berlin, 49, 96, 113, 118, 136, 141
Berthold of Henneberg, archbishop of Mainz, 61-2
Bethmann-Hollweg, 130, 131, 133
Bismarck, 110, 112, 114-27, 154, 157
Black Forest, 29
Bohemia, 1, 2, 29, 30, 41, 42, 46, 53-7, 60, 69, 75
Böhmer, Johann Friedrich, 110 *n*
Boleslav III of Poland (1102-1139), 41
Boniface, Saint, 5, 9

Bosnia-Herzegovina, 133
Bouvines, battle of (1214), 23, 37
Bowring, Dr. John, 119 *n*
Brabant, 57
Brandenburg, 41-7, 49, 53-4, 56, 67, 77, 79, 84
Brandenburg-Prussia, 81, 91 *n*; rise of, 95-100
Brant, Sebastian, 60
Bremen, 74, 141
Breslau, 41
Brest-Litovsk, Treaty of (1918), 135, 136, 143
Bruchsal, 87
Brüning, 149
Brunswick, 78
Bülow, 130, 131
Burgundy, 4, 18, 19, 30, 36, 37, 39, 57; acquisition by Austria (1477), 58-61; free county of (*Freigrafschaft, Franche-Comté*), 39, 83
Buxtehude, Dietrich, 85.

Cambrai, 39
Campo Formio, Peace of (1797), 102
Caprivi, 125-6, 128, 130
Carlsbad Decrees (1819), 112
Casimir the Great of Poland (1333-1370), 41
Castlereagh, 108
Catherine II of Russia, 100
Catholic League, 69, 70
Centre Party, 137, 148, 150 *n*
Chamberlain, Neville, 151
Charlemagne, 5, 6; legend of, 102
Charles IV (1346-1378), 31-2, 41, 51-4, 63 *n*
Charles V (1519-1556), 60, 61, 63, 64, 65, 67, 68, 69, 72
Charles VII of France, 40
Charles Martel, 4
Charles the Bold, Duke of Burgundy (1467-1477), 57, 58
Charles the Great, *see* Charlemagne
Clausewitz, 118
Clemenceau, 142, 144, 160
Clement VI (1342-1352), 31
Cleves, duchy of, 96
Clovis (485-511), 2, 4
Cologne, 24, 69; electorate of, 58
Communist Party, 146, 148, 150 *n*
Confederation of the Rhine, 102
Confoederatio cum principibus ecclesiasticis (1220), 25
Conrad I (911-918), 7
Conrad II (1024-1039), 10, 11

161